The Love of Italy

JONATHAN KEATES

octopus

LUCE

COELESTI CRESCAT

Ex Libris
CHELTENHAM LADIES'
COLLEGE

The Love of Italy

CONTENTS

PUGLIA
(APULIA)

Bari

Brindisi

Matera

Taranto

Lecce

CATA

senza

CALABRIA

Catanzaro

IONIAN SEA

Endpapers: A shop front in Verona.
Page 1: Gondola, symbol of Venice.
Pages 2–3: Fishermen, southern Italy.
Pages 6–7: Burano, Venice.

First published in 1980 by Octopus Books Limited,
59 Grosvenor Street, London, W.1.

ISBN 0 7064 1237 0

© 1980 Octopus Books Limited

Produced by Mandarin Publishers Limited,
22a Westlands Road, Quarry Bay, Hong Kong.

Printed in Hong Kong

FOREWORD
by John Julius Norwich

There is no analyzing love. Love for a foreign country — not for one's own, which has to do with home, and family, and roots, and is something quite different — is like love for another person: there is an element of magic about it. If you could define the feeling logically, it wouldn't be love.

Yet Italy is probably the best beloved country in the world, and — magic apart — it seems worth enquiring why, for example, Dr Johnson should have written over two hundred years ago that 'a man who has not been in Italy is always conscious of an inferiority' and why, for a good hundred years before that — long, long before anybody ever thought about beaches, or sunshine, or even the beauty of landscape (which was itself largely an eighteenth-century discovery) — young men from other, less favoured climes were already crossing the Alps in search of education and enlightenment.

The reason for this long history of pilgrimage is that the Italians have not only contributed incomparably more than any other people to the civilization of the West; they have quite simply revolutionized it — and done so not once, but twice, first through Ancient Rome and then with the Renaissance. Without those two tremendous moulding forces, where would the western world be today? Yet even these, I suspect, are mere manifestations of some deeper cause — a burning, driving, intellectual and artistic energy that gave its possessors no rest.

Today, it would take a lifetime to see even half what this miraculous land has to offer. And that brings us to the next question that every visitor finds himself asking sooner or later: how can there be so much splendour, so many breathtaking towns and cities, palaces and churches, paintings and statues and works of art? The answer lies, paradoxically, in Italy's greatest failure — to unite. It is all too easy to forget that this land has been one country for little more than a century, that before the *Risorgimento* it was, as Metternich put it, 'a geographical expression', a jumble of states of varying strengths and sizes, sharing a language and a vague feeling of *italianità,* but little else. To the people this disunity brought much suffering and distress, but to its artistic heritage the benefit was incalculable. Even today Italy remains the most decentralized country in Europe; it is a country where every major city is a historic capital, with a character, a style, a tradition of its own.

All lovers of Italy understand this, and have their own favourites. My own list would include Verona, where at night in the Piazza dei Signori time seems to have stood still for five centuries; Cefalù in Sicily, where the immense Byzantine mosaic of Christ Pantocrator in the apse of the cathedral remains for me the most moving portrait of the Redeemer in all Christian art; S. Clemente in Rome, where over a thousand years of Christian history are miraculously encapsulated in a single building; and, above all, it goes without saying, the entire city of Venice, every brick and stone of it, the crowning masterpiece of the western world, on which — were I ever called upon to defend our civilization — I should rest my case.

If Mr Keates's list is different from mine, so much the better. He writes with both scholarship and enthusiasm — why is that combination so rare? — and has produced a book which, helped by magnificent photography, brings Italy alive before us. And no wonder; for here, if ever there was one, is a labour of love.

John Julius Norwich

The Diversity of Piedmont and Lombardy

Superfically, nothing could be further removed from the popular image of Italy than the northern regions of Piedmont and Lombardy. There are blue skies and sunshine, certainly, but these are softened and subtly influenced by the atmosphere and colours of an alpine landscape. It is a landscape with gentle rains, swirling mists, brilliant white snow slopes and the jagged scarps of dark mountain peaks. Elements of suddenness and surprise dominate everything here. Anyone lucky enough to make their first descent into Italy by car or, better still, by train, will notice this at once. The little valleys on either side of the fast-flowing torrents carry the promise of abundant fertility in their strings of vines and rich pastures. Such ripeness blooms in the rich soil of the plains of Lombardy, which have fields of rice, wheat and maize criss-crossed with avenues of poplars.

The mountains themselves have been an important factor in Italy's relationships with the rest of Europe. To generations of invaders and travellers, from Hannibal in the 3rd century BC to today's tourists, they have offered both a temptation and a barrier. 'Cross us,' they have always seemed to say, 'and look at what lies beyond – but never count on coming back.' When viewed in the distance from Venice to Turin their outlines can seem gloomy and forbidding. Many have come down from these mountains never to return. It is not surprising that past travellers often lingered for months or even years in Italy rather than face the arduous journey home.

Nowadays, however, the slopes, moraines and glaciers of Mont Blanc, Monte Rosa and the Gran Paradiso are less willingly left behind. Saulze d'Oulx, Sestriere and Macugnaga offer fashionable winter sporting activities to the prosperous industrialists of Turin. Carloads of Milanese set off for weekend skiing at Bormio, Stelvio and Santa Caterina. Wild nature, for which Italy often seems to have little time, is given a chance to flourish here in the Gran Paradiso National Park (once, ironically, a royal hunting preserve). Home of chamois and marmot, the park also offers a last refuge for the rare alpine ibex.

Eastwards along the alpine fringes lie the serenely beautiful lakes. Maggiore is the largest, its northern end crossing the Swiss border. Exotic plants flourish in the gardens of the grand villas and hotels at Stresa and Pallanza. In the lake itself lie the four islands that bear the historic and powerful name of Borromeo, the family who still own them. The Borromeo palace, surrounded by terraced gardens, stands on Isola Bella, formerly a bare rock until it was turfed and planted in the 17th century. Lake Como is the longest of the lakes and, many hold, the most appealing. It divides into two arms, with the westernmost culminating in the cathedral town of Como. Iseo is the smallest. It is surrounded with pretty towns and villages, such as Bossico and Lovere, where the witty and eccentric 18th-century English letter-writer, Lady Mary Wortley Montagu, found a home. Garda, last of all, has an attractive southern fringe, close to Verona, whose Roman citizens favoured it as a resort. Among them was the poet Catullus, who immortalized the Sirmio peninsula (which juts out into the lake and has caves named after him) in one of his shorter poems.

PREVIOUS PAGES *The view from Stresa, a resort on the western shore of Lake Maggiore, looking towards the Borromean Islands which lie in the middle of the lake. Lake Maggiore divides the northern fringes of Lombardy and Piedmont, and its northern end is in Switzerland.*

BELOW LEFT *Dotted with attractive little towns and villages, the long, slender arms of Lake Como link Lombardy with the high Alps. The brilliant colours of the lake landscape make an ideal introduction to Italy, and Como is surrounded by high mountains as well as the luxuriant vegetation which also lines the shores of Lake Maggiore. Green groves of chestnut and walnut contrast with dark cypress and grey olive. Palm and ilex offset the bright-toned semi-tropical vegetation of villa gardens.*

BELOW RIGHT *The lush terraces of Isola Bella, most famous of the Borromean Islands, reflect the wealth and taste of the Milanese Borromeo family.*

RIGHT *Gran Paradiso, a National Park, was once a royal hunting ground. It rises from the Valle d'Aosta and offers spectacular views.*

BELOW Modern Milan presents a layered mixture of cities. The Roman core centres on the flamboyant mediaeval Duomo, the third largest church in Europe. It was begun in 1386 for Gian Galeazzo, member of the powerful and ambitious Visconti clan, who had family connections with Edward III of England. Building continued in the 15th and 16th centuries, and the façade was only finished in 1809, by order of Napoleon. The cathedral stands at one end of a great paved esplanade, where the Milanese come to stroll in the early evening and talk over the events of the day, *RIGHT*.

BELOW RIGHT The modern shops and offices of one of the world's busiest cities – the second largest in Italy and the most important economically – confront the Duomo. Between them stands the statue of King Victor Emmanuel of Savoy, first king of united Italy. It was designed in 1896 by Ercole Rosa. Renaissance and Baroque palaces, with façades of pink, yellow and brown, line the neighbouring streets and squares, making the lively heart of the city also its most attractive district. Fashionable shops and cafés abound in the city centre, as do picture galleries and museums (including the Brera, the Ambrosian Library, the Poldi-Pezzoli and the Gallery of Modern Art) where masterpieces by Mantegna, Bellini, Leonardo da Vinci and others may be seen. In the surrounding suburbs industries such as textiles and chemicals are important trades.

Piedmont, 'the foot of the mountain,' is the name given not only to Italy's western border but to the ancient kingdom of which it once formed the heart. It was here, on the very edge of Italy, that the idea of a united country took solid shape. King Victor Emmanuel and his minister, Count Cavour, as crafty as he was patriotic, created the new nation in a series of diplomatic manoeuvres in the 19th century. Perhaps because of their closeness to France the Piedmontese have thus always taken seriously the business of being Italian. The regional dialect, however, carries strong Gallic touches and French was the language most readily used by the royalty and nobility of the old kingdom.

Even the food has a distinctly French flavour. This may be experienced in such dishes as *bagna cauda*, a spicy hot dip for raw vegetables; *lepre Piemontese*, hare cooked in wine, herbs and bitter chocolate; and *fonduta*, the local version of the typical Swiss cheese fondue. The wines, moreover, are the best in Italy, if still little known abroad. Everyone has come across the red Tuscan Chianti in its familiar straw *fiasco*, but how many, before they come to Piedmont, have ever sampled the rich and full-bodied Barolo, Barbera and Grignolino?

The stern individuality (some might say over-seriousness) of the Piedmontese is mirrored in the rugged and defensive look of their towns and villages. Aosta, oldest of the region's cities, is girdled with its Roman walls. Its ancient name was Augusta Praetoria.

Rome's imprint is still seen in Augustus's own triumphal arch as well as in the magnificent rear wall of the theatre. Ivrea has a four-towered medieval castle, built for the warrior Count Amadeus VI of Savoy in 1358. Asti, famous for its sweet, fizzy white wine, is almost a guide-book to local history. Romanesque and Gothic churches jostle with Renaissance and Baroque palaces.

No city, however, better sums up the Piedmontese achievement than the former royal capital of Turin. The people of this city are sometimes described as 'false and courteous'. 'False' is a little unfair. 'Courteous' seems much more just, since the royal house of Savoy and its courtiers always looked towards their more sophisticated French counterparts for a positive lead in good manners. The city's layout reflects the growth in importance of the powerful buffer state between France and the territories of northern Italy that were ruled by Austria.

Turin's plan is almost American in its grid of rigid streets, which converge now and then upon spectacular squares. 'The finest village in the whole world' was the comment of the 18th century French philosopher Montesquieu. The new capital he saw was partially the work of the talented Sicilian, Filippo Juvarra. Beyond the city limits Juvarra's genius for romantic magnificence was given free rein in the royal hunting lodge at Stupinigi, which is decorated with frescoes by Carl Van Loo, and in the Basilica of Superga, crowning a hilltop to the south.

The world knows Turin, however, for a very different reason. Italy, which means pizza and spaghetti to some, opera and art to others, spells Fiat to the world's motorists. Here, during the early decades of this century, the Agnelli family built up their vast automobile empire. They soon expanded into other European markets with a series of sleek, capably modelled family cars. So heavily concentrated an industry has, of course, made the city among the country's most prosperous. The incentives offered to migrant workers from the impoverished south, however, have created in Turin a floating community with problems.

A similar commercial boom has attracted southerners to Milan, the capital of Lombardy and one of Europe's biggest cities. It sprawls across the plain for mile after suburban mile. No one has ever ranked Milan among Italy's more appealing provincial centres. In winter drizzle or fog, few places seem quite so uniformly depressing. But Milanese life has always possessed a sophisticated vitality that has drawn visitors to the city regardless of its noise and grime. Apart from its obvious importance as a world trade capital, with yearly fairs, conferences and exhibitions, it has lively traditions of music and theatre and two of the best art collections in Italy.

Roman, medieval and Renaissance rulers all left their mark on Milan. Paradoxically, though, it was under Austrian rule in the 18th and 19th centuries that it truly flourished. Vigorous literary and intellectual activity threw up many outstanding figures.

The most famous building in Milan, the celebrated La Scala opera house, opened its doors towards the close of the 18th century. Not far away, in the street where the poet and novelist Alessandro Manzoni lived, we can visit the Poldi-Pezzoli museum. Named after its owner, the collection and its palace were given to the city in 1879. A private art gallery is nearly always more interesting than a public display, reflecting as it does a marked individual taste. The Poldi-Pezzoli, with its choice examples of Florentine and Venetian painting and portraits from the hand of the Bergamasque Fra Galgario, is no exception. Close by, nevertheless, is Milan's own Brera gallery, arguably the best representative national collection in Italy. This features canvases from all the major schools as well as such appealing minor talents as that of the 19th century Milanese portraitist Francesco Hayez.

His ringletted countesses and stiff-collared senators can easily be imagined attending a stirring evening of opera by Rossini or Donizetti at La Scala. This fine old auditorium has seen a number of triumphs and disasters, culminating in memorable performances by

Maria Callas, greatest of modern prima donnas. A night at La Scala is never dull or disappointing. Elsewhere in the city the Piccolo Teatro di Milano offers the very best in modern Italian theatre. Shakespeare, Goldoni, Chekhov and Brecht form the core of a wide international repertoire.

FAR LEFT *The Duomo's many marble statues and 135 fretted pinnacles represent the most ambitious Gothic design in the whole of Italy.* RIGHT *The Teatro alla Scala, built in 1778 by the architect Piermarini, is venerated by the world's opera lovers. Six tiers of private boxes form the classic horseshoe-shaped auditorium, which can accommodate more than 3,000 people. During performance intervals, members of the audience can visit the theatre's own museum and art gallery.* BELOW *The Galleria Vittorio Emmanuele, Europe's grandest shopping arcade, adorned with fresco and mosaic, was built in 1856–7. Its architect, Mengoni, fell to his death from the scaffolding while adding the finishing touches.*

Milan's own province of Lombardy comprises two distinct geographical regions. The broad, flat plain lying along the north bank of the Po meets the mountains at the shores of Como and Garda. Few people are ever likely to visit Lombardy for its countryside of chessboard fields and regimented poplars, but its towns, each with a definite personality, are not to be ignored. Pavia, for instance, has a strongly felt character arising from its former role as the capital of the Longobards. This powerful Germanic tribe, whose name means 'long beards,' settled in this part of Italy at the fall of the Roman empire, and it became known as Longobardia or Lombardia. Here Lanfranc, the first great Archbishop of Canterbury under the Normans, was born. He studied at Pavia's law school, which later became a noted university.

Like many Italian cities, Bergamo began life as a free commune. It was eventually drawn into the medieval power politics of the great northern Italian families. In 1428 it fell to the Venetian republic and became one of the cornerstones of Venice's mainland domains. Sturdy Lombard independence, challenging northern invaders, played its part here when

Bergamo rebelled against the Austrians in the 19th century. There is a defiant, proud look to this place, which rolls across the hill and down to the plain, with the Alps behind. No wonder that the town produced two of the most forceful talents in 16th-century painting, Lotto and Moroni. Lorenzo Lotto is best known for capturing the fleeting, preoccupied expressions of young women, scholars and noblemen, and for imaginative religious groups. Visitors to the National Gallery in London can see there *The Tailor* by Giovanni Battista Moroni. The penetrating glance of the man who raises his eyes from cutting out a length of cloth is echoed in the faces of the aristocratic Lombard citizens who sat for one of the truly great portrait artists of his age.

Pictures by Lotto and Moroni are to be seen in the Accademia Carrara, one of the best of Italy's smaller galleries. In Bergamo's cathedral is the elegant Colleoni Chapel, designed by the architect Amadeo in 1476. Here is buried the great *condottiere* (soldier of fortune), Bartolommeo Colleoni. His statue stands outside the church of San Giovanni e Paolo in Venice. Colleoni represented a particular late medieval phenomenon in Italy's

political unrest. He was employed as a professional military leader by the Venetian state and profited accordingly. Venice commemorated him with an equestrian statue by Andrea Verrocchio. In Bergamo, horse and rider are by the German artist Siry.

Bergamo was also the birthplace of Gaetano Donizetti, composer of several of the world's most popular operas. After a highly successful career, reaching a peak in music dramas such as *Lucia di Lammermoor* and comedies like *L'Elisir d'Amore*, Donizetti began to lose his reason and died insane in 1848. The town has not forgotten him, however, and the house where he was born is now a museum and study centre. Donizetti's music, lyrical, romantic and tuneful, appealed to the revolutionary Italy of his day. Some of his melodies were actually adapted to political verses. As with Verdi, people saw anti-Austrian analogies in some of his operas.

Nowhere in Lombardy was more resentful of this foreign occupation than Brescia, due east from Milan across the plain. In 1849 Brescia held out with incredible bravery against a prolonged Austrian siege by the fierce, sadistic General Haynau. He probably

deserved his English nickname of 'General Hyena,' for his reprisals were extremely cruel, but his tribute to the indomitable Brescians is worth recording. 'Give me a thousand of these fellows', he said, 'and I would march on Paris tomorrow.'

Brescia has had its fair share of Lombard individualists. Centuries before Haynau's praise the monk Arnold fearlessly criticized the flagrant worldliness of the Church. For this, in 1155, he was hanged. With these traditions of holding its head high, the town valiantly withstood wartime bombing in the 1940s. The splendid Piazza della Loggia is a witness of this survival. The Loggia itself is a composite achievement by various Rennaissance architects. These include Sansovino, better known as designer of the library in the Piazzetta in Venice, and Palladio, a visitor from Vicenza. Rich in fine squares, Brescia also boasts a grandiose cathedral alongside a Romanesque round church, which is borne on eight pillars and dates from the early 12th century. The city's theatre has been owned by its box-holders since it was founded in the early 18th century – a state of affairs once common enough but rare today.

TOP LEFT *The great Gallery of Antiquities in the Garden Palace at Sabbioneta, on the fringes of Lombardy and Emilia. The haunting loveliness of this little town is enhanced by its decay. Created by the Gonzaga family of nearby Mantua during the 16th century, Sabbioneta was intended as a small but perfect model town on ideal Renaissance lines, and it became for a time the centre of a refined court. It was soon abandoned, however, and is now a superb ghost town of palaces, churches and theatres.*

ABOVE *Bergamo, on the other hand, is a lively, modern city with a picturesque old upper town surrounded by 16th-century Venetian walls. Within these walls are many witnesses of a prosperous past, among them the ornate 15th-century Colleoni Chapel, shown here. The design, by Giovanni Antonio Amadeo, fuses Renaissance and Romanesque; the façade is covered with multicoloured marble and delicate sculptures.*

LEFT *A fiddle by Antonio Stradivari (1644–1737), also known as Stradivarius, symbolizes Cremona's traditions of violin making, which reached the peak of perfection during the 17th and 18th centuries.*

Finally let us visit a place that never really seems to belong in Lombardy at all. Mantua, once a proud capital of an independent duchy, lies in the marshlands of the Mincio, a tributary of the Po. Its rulers were the Gonzaga family, as colourful and dangerous a clan as Renaissance Italy ever produced. They had a liking for luxurious palaces, and these survive today in the enormous central sprawl of the Palazzo Ducale and the elegant seclusion of the Palazzo del Te. The former contains the Camera degli Sposi, Andrea Mantegna's striking celebration of the glories of Lodovico Gonzaga and his consort, Barbara of Brandenburg. The variety of Renaissance court life is suggested not only by the riding school and the theatre, but also by special apartments for the court dwarfs. A reminder of more sinister matters is given by the cage hanging from the Torre della Gabbia, where prisoners were exposed to the crowd.

Mantua became an Austrian garrison town in 1708 and the Gonzaga fortunes collapsed. But for a final memory of this weird, silent city of court ghosts, sitting amid glassy lakes on the fringes of Lombardy and Emilia, there is the Teatro Scientifico. Part of the Accademia Virgiliana in a modest side-street, this is the work of Antonio Bibbiena and was begun in 1769. It is not strictly speaking a theatre for entertainment but a place for academic demonstrations. Nevertheless, as a piece of theatre architecture, with its flowing lines of marble balustrading and broad proscenium arch, it has no parallel anywhere else in the world.

Former glories mark the Ducal city of Mantua. The Gonzaga family ruled it with a mixture of ruthlessness and extravagance, and patronized artists of the calibre of Pisanello, Mantegna and, later, Rubens. The palaces and pavilions of the town reflect generations of discernment and good taste in an exceptionally gifted Renaissance family. LEFT An interior of the Ducal Palace which is composed of more than 450 rooms, as well as numerous squares, courtyards and gardens.

In the Castello San Giorgio, a 14th-century fortress which is part of the palace, is the Camera degli Sposi with a series of frescoes by Andrea Mantegna (painted between 1465–74). One in the series shows Lodovico Gonzaga with his family, ABOVE. Mantegna's knowledge of foreshortening creates an impression of space in his work and gives his figures a sculptural quality. Nearby, on the façade of the Palazzo Broletto, is a statue of the poet Virgil, born near Mantua in 70 BC.

Echoes of Venetian Glory

Lions no longer run wild in Europe but you will find them still all over the Mediterranean, adorning historic relics from Lisbon to Greece and Jerusalem. One particular lion is to be seen on the walls of fortified cities on the Aegean islands between Greece and Turkey and on the coast of Yugoslavia that borders the Adriatic Sea. It has wings and holds a book and sometimes carries a sword. It is the lion of St Mark the Evangelist, historic symbol of the city and former republic of Venice.

Everything about Venice begins and ends in romance, dream or fantasy. Plain facts alone will not answer the riddle of how it was founded in the 5th century by refugees who built their crude homes on mudflats, or how it became the centre of a powerful republic that ruled the Mediterranean. Venice and its republic were a Christian outpost against the Turks and conquered Constantinople, Crete and Cyprus. Its merchant fleet traded in gemstones, silks and spices from the East, and Venetian conquests extended inland almost to the gates of Milan. The city became the envy and delight of Europe. From the 15th century political decline set in and the republic finally came to an end in the last years of the 18th century. Yet it was in this period of reduced international sway that some of Venice's most beautiful buildings were erected and some of her most gifted painters and playwrights flourished. The magnitude of their achievement can still be witnessed today.

The approach to Venice is magical. On a sunny day the visitor who comes from the mainland by car, bus or train sees the city appear like a shimmering mirage on water. From the air you can see its weird shape. It could be thought to resemble a guitar, or a huge flat fish complete with fins, tail and mouth. The train carries you in by the back door, as it were. Step out of the railway station and you are on the edge of the Grand Canal, with elaborately decorated Baroque and Rococo churches all around. By sea, from

Greece or Yugoslavia perhaps, what could be more marvellous than to watch Venice pushing up its domes and pinnacles over the horizon of the lagoon?

Few of the many thousands of tourists who visit Venice each year ever remain long enough. A trip down the Grand Canal by gondola or vaporetto, the purchase of a souvenir from the Rialto, an ice-cream in St Mark's Square and that, too often, is thought sufficient. The uniqueness of Venice, however, can never be fully experienced in a day or two. The city has to be savoured. Its pace, unhurried by cars or bicycles, is a measured one. Venice has a rhythm unlike that of any other city, one which takes in countless lei-

surely walks through narrow lanes and visits to churches and museums, broken by pauses for a cup of coffee or a glass of wine at a bar. The pulse is entirely human in this city with the largest concentration of man-made beauty in the world.

From early on, Venetian life was marked by spectacle and extravagance. The grand processions to St Mark's Cathedral in the great days of the republic gave way to lavish carnivals, expensive opera and other theatrical displays. Accordingly, the siting of churches and palaces on the numerous squares and canals was often chosen in defiance of convention or even good taste for the sake of a brilliant effect. Such opulent gestures con-

PREVIOUS PAGES The Piazzetta in Venice, with the Doges' Palace on the left, the Old Library on the right, and the lion of St Mark in the centre of the picture, looks towards the Island of San Giorgio. The 15th-century palace, both the seat of government and the residence of the doges, symbolized the power and glory of Venice. INSET Venice from the air, showing the Grand Canal winding through it.
BELOW A row of moored gondolas makes a uniquely Venetian scene. Nowadays used merely for pleasure trips, the gondola was once the city's main form of water transport. The boats were originally painted black, to comply with a 15th-century senatorial law, and are usually still that colour.

PREVIOUS PAGES The basilica of St Mark, whose five large doorways face St Mark's Square, is built on the plan of a Greek Cross and has five domes of different heights. It was begun in 976 AD, in order to house the relics of St Mark the Evangelist, Venice's patron saint. Looted from Alexandria in 828, his body was brought to the city as part of a typical merchant enterprise, and the whole cathedral is indeed enriched with the spoils of mediaeval raids and expeditions. The interior, with its rich and exotic semi-Oriental designs and Byzantine mosaics, is indicative of the success of the city's merchant ventures in the eastern Mediterranean. One such was the acquisition of Cyprus from Queen Caterina Cornaro, celebrated, LEFT, by the annual regatta on the Grand Canal on the first Sunday in September. This is only one of many festive events held in Venice throughout the year. The Venetians love pomp and ceremony, and festivals and carnivals seem extremely appropriate events to stage against the beautiful backcloth of ancient buildings. lapped by the water of 150 canals.

The canals carry a variety of craft, such as the light sandalo, ABOVE, *and the gondola, one of which is shown passing the Bridge of Sighs,* RIGHT. *Named from the supposed sighs of condemned men, the Bridge of Sighs linked the court-rooms of the Doges' palace with the adjacent prisons.*

tained within the limits of a city bounded by marshes and tides exert a profound effect on the receptive visitor.

Venice is one of the few places in Italy that has a fair share of ghost stories. Writers, painters and composers have all been inspired by the romantic gloom and melancholy so easily imparted by a city whose splendours derive exclusively from the past. It is a collection of splendours that is, however, under attack, now more than ever before, by a combination of rising water-levels, sinking foundations and atmospheric pollution from mainland industries. A major attempt has been launched to prevent the collapse of the city into the muddy lagoon from which it rose, but obstacles hinder concerted action. Money is one, local politics intrude, and many Italians point to the apathy of the Venetians themselves, leaving old houses empty in this city, where house prices are higher than anywhere else in Italy.

LEFT Life in Venice is carried out among a warren of alleys, lanes and canals, many of which have been given bizarre and evocative names, such as 'the Assassins', 'the Spice Shop', 'Oysters', 'Sausages', 'Rosemary', 'the Nobles' Casino', 'the Love of Friends', and others. The exotic names indicate that this is a meeting point for East and West, one of the characteristics for which Venice is famed. Market stalls stand next to palaces; and, though the city has rail links with the mainland, many essential goods such as fruit and vegetables are brought in and delivered by boat.
RIGHT An essential feature of the city skyline is the bold outline of the church of S. Maria della Salute (Our Lady of Health). The church was a great favourite with visiting painters such as Turner and Bonington. It was built in 1631 by Baldassare Longhena, at the entrance to the Grand Canal, and is a magnificent fulfilment of a pledge by the Venetian state, following a terrible epidemic of plague. The church has a huge interior: its dome surmounts an octagonal ground plan, and its main doors are right on the water's edge. A painting by Tintoretto, the Marriage at Cana, is in the sacristy. On the left of the church is a 17th-century seminary. At the end of the land strip on the south side of the Grand Canal (the Punte della Salute) is the Dogana da Mar, built in 1682, former customs house of the republic and still in use today. There is a revolving statue of Fortune mounted on one of its small towers, which acts as a weather vane.

In the old days Venice unquestionably took more than she gave, but none of the towns and cities of the Venetians is without her imprint. Verona, for example, has numerous examples, although it is of earlier empires and rulers that her larger buildings most vividly remind us. The huge Arena, the third largest existing from Roman times, provides an impressive setting for opera and ballet performances in summer. The walls of Castelvecchio, built for a medieval tyrant, now house a superb museum. Here, as in Venice itself, can be seen the brilliance and boldness that characterized the so-called 'Venetian' school of painting. It was a flowering of genius that produced, at the turn of the 15th and 16th centuries, painters such as Giorgione, Bellini and Titian, and Verona's own artistic giant, Paolo Caliari, known as Veronese.

What these painters saw, in terms of light and landscape, can be seen today. To the north are the outlines of the Dolomites, from whose foothills Titian set out to court the patronage of wealthy Venetians. On the plains lie small towns such as Treviso or Castelfranco, home of Giorgione, who depicted its yellow and brown roofs and towers in several of his paintings. In the lush green foothills between Verona and the mountains there is, here and there, a place like Conegliano, whose own painter, Cima, used its skies, fields and walls in his religious works.

ABOVE Verona's varied history is mirrored in the layout of the city's streets, on what is fundamentally a Roman plan, as well as in its mediaeval and Renaissance palaces. The city in which Shakespeare's Romeo and Juliet is set stands on the River Adige in an area of cypress-covered hills. The setting is no less than Verona deserves, for it is, after Venice, the most important centre of the arts in Venetia. The architecture of the city in every way matches its fine setting. There are superb squares, including the picturesque Piazza delle Erbe which marks the original forum, Romanesque churches, and a vast amphitheatre in the Piazza Bra, the third largest in the Roman world.

RIGHT San Zeno in Verona, begun in 1139, is one of the finest Romanesque churches in northern Italy. The interior of the church has a keel-shaped roof. There is a beautiful triptych (1459) of the Madonna and Saints by Mantegna at the high altar. Napoleon found this painting so attractive that he took it, but it was returned, in part, after his fall. (The panels of the predella can be found in the Louvre in Paris and in the museum at Tours.) There are 13th-century statues of Christ and the Apostles on the chancel barrier.

BELOW The doors, decorated with brazen plates showing crudely vivid reliefs of scenes from the Old and New Testaments, are probably older than the church itself.

The medieval heart of Verona, the background for Shakespeare's *Romeo and Juliet*, is echoed in the wonderful frescoes by Giotto that decorate the interior of the Scrovegni Chapel in Padua. An ancient university town, Padua achieved fame in the early history of medical research. Galileo taught there, so did Vesalius, an important figure in anatomy, and the physiologist Fallopius. William Harvey, who discovered that blood circulated around the body, took his degree at Padua in 1602. In many eras students exerted a dominant role in the life of the city. Padua was in the forefront of revolutionary activity in the 19th century and it is still noted as a centre of political and social dissent.

As if to remind us of its turbulent past, the Piazza del Santo contains Donatello's equestrian statue of Erasmo da Narni, known as Gattamelata, who was a mercenary in the pay of Venice. This can be contrasted, however, with the gentleness of Padua's saint, St Anthony. He was a native of Lisbon and came under the influence of St Francis. After settling in Padua he sought to persuade people to care for their natural surroundings. St Anthony has become the patron saint of the helpless and the absent-minded, and his tomb in the basilica of Sant'Antonio is hung with strange and sometimes macabre offerings.

The landscape of the Venetian plain may be thought dull, but it is made interesting by the handsome villas that were built by city nobles as country retreats for the summer. From their mansions at harvest-time they would supervise the gathering of stores for winter, attend to business on their estates, and collect rents. In style these villas are a typically Italian mixture of the grand and the practical. They were often built so that the lower floor could serve as farm-sheds and offices, and the upper floors had large, airy apartments for family entertaining. The plan is similar to the palaces in Venice, the lowest storey of which might originally have been used for unloading merchandise from canal boats.

In designing these villas no architect did more to fuse imagination with a respect for the past than Andrea Palladio. His influence on building was great and is still evident today. In the early 17th century English travellers were deeply impressed by the delicacy and restraint of the design in Palladio's houses, such as the Villa Capra, called the Rotonda, at Vicenza and the Villa Foscari at Oriago on the banks of the Brenta.

Vicenza is, above all, Palladio's city. It is a place of broad streets and ample squares set among the rolling slopes of the Berici mountains. Apart from the palaces by Palladio and his pupil Scamozzi, the town contains his final masterpiece, the Teatro Olimpico, which was begun in 1580. Built of wood and stucco it recreates in modified form a Roman theatre, and has curved tiers of seats and a fixed backdrop of a square with radiating streets.

Anyone with time to spare at Vicenza should go up to the nearby hillsides and visit the churches and villas on the outskirts of the city. A notable attraction is the enchanting Valmarana dei Nani, a 17th-century villa adorned with frescoes by the last truly inspired Venetian painters in the grand manner, Giovanni Battista Tiepolo and his son Giandomenico. The suddenness with which these hills rise from the plain recalls the much more abrupt summits near Padua to the south, the Colli Euganei. The hills around Vicenza have a close similarity to those of Tuscany, being host to neat, compact little towns and numerous health resorts and spas.

RIGHT Padua was an important cultural, commercial and religious centre even before the time of the Holy Roman Empire. It is known as the city of saints and scholars. The University of Padua was founded in 1222 by the Emperor Frederick II, and by the end of the 17th century had 6,000 students. Galileo was at one time a professor there, and among its most famous students were Dante, Petrarch and Tasso.

ABOVE Frescoes by Giotto in the Scrovegni Chapel. The chapel is also known as the Madonna dell' Arena. The great Florentine painter began this cycle of frescoes in 1306. The pictures show scenes from the lives of Christ and the Virgin, centring on the Last Judgment painted over the entrance arch. Especially moving in their ability to suggest intense drama through a carefully controlled simplicity of line are panels such as the Betrayal of Christ and the Last Supper, BELOW LEFT. Enrico Scrovegni, who is buried here, built the chapel as an atonement for his father's activities as a usurer.

The Dolomites define the northern boundary of the region, and Italy itself. These eastern alps take their name from the French geologist Gratet de Dolomieu, and it was Dolomieu who gave his own name to their peculiar pinkish limestone. The Dolomites draw holiday-makers in their thousands every year. Cortina D'Ampezzo is the largest and most popular of several skiing resorts. Botanists and walkers are also attracted by these mountains, rich in alpine flora and rare species of auricula, saxifrage and campanula.

The glaciers, craggy peaks and rock-faces, the pine woods, tarns and lakes are all reminiscent of the neighbouring Tyrol, across the border in Austria. In this frontier region, known as the Alto Adige, German is as commonly spoken as Italian. Towns such as Bolzano and Merano have a strongly Austrian character, most clearly seen in the design of their houses with steeply pitched bargeboard roofs. During World War I this was a hotly contested border and allegiance is divided still. Austria's relationship with Italy has always been a sensitive issue. It owes its origins to mistrust arising from the period when the whole of Venetia-Lombardy was a province of the Hapsburgs. Liberation was achieved only in 1866.

The uneasy fusion of the two nationalities is felt most strongly in Trieste, which was never officially part of Italy until the mid-1950s. Commanding the curve of the Adriatic into Yugoslavia, Trieste retains a strange, unique atmosphere. This was once Austria's largest seaport and after World War II it was administered by Allied powers. In 1954 the city came under the control of Italy. So, although Italian is the main language and Italian forms of government are used, the city still seems very much a part of the old Hapsburg empire.

Between Trieste and Venice stretches Italy's most northerly region, Fruili. It is an area with an individuality marked by a fascinating dialect and a ripe tradition of poetry and folksong. Its capital is Udine, which was recently shaken by severe earthquakes, as it has been many times in the past. Yet, despite damage, it still preserves the essence of a fine old city. And here in the Piazza della Liberta, as at Padua, Treviso and Verona, is the lion of St Mark the Evangelist, symbol of Venice.

*LEFT The Dolomites, Italy's eastern Alps, rise more suddenly from the green wooded foothills than their westerly neighbours. Their distinctive landscape is made up of steep, rugged rocks which descend to smooth slopes of alpine pastures, conifers and crops. The fauna of this region is quite varied and one can find chamois, deer, royal eagles, hawks and woodcock in the coniferous forests. Popular with winter sporting enthusiasts, the Dolomites are equally attractive to botanists for their profusion of rare wild flowers and alpine plants: the fields are covered with crocus, campanula and edelweiss. The fertile valleys support market gardening and the cultivation of vines.
Most of the Dolomites are formed of limestone rocks. The reason why these rocks are called 'Dolomites' is that a French geologist called Gratet de Dolomieu was the first person to carry out extensive studies on their formation at the end of the 18th century. One of the best ways to see the greatness of the Dolomites is to travel along the Dolomite Road, which was the main route for Renaissance merchants travelling from Venice to Germany.*

ABOVE The Ponte Coperto (covered bridge) over the River Brenta at Bassano. The bridge has been destroyed many times in its history, but it has always been rebuilt. The present bridge (1945) is a reconstruction of the original version. Bassano lies close to Tyrolean Austria and this is evident in the bridge's architecture. Bassano's most famous inhabitant was the artist Jacopa da Ponte, who died in 1952. He founded Bassanism, a style characterized by bright colours. Bassano itself is renowned for two things: pottery and brandy. The neighbouring area was the scene for one of Napoleon's most spectacular victories over the Austrians. East of Bassano lies Asolo, in whose cemetery lies the English Victorian poet, Robert Browning, and the famous Italian actress, Duse. Nearby Monte Grappa offers spectacular views of the whole area, and, when the weather permits, it is possible to see as far as Venice and Trieste. The view also takes in the valley of the Brenta and the Venetian plain. The mountain was of strategic importance in the First World War, and a nearby ossuary contains the bones of 25,000 soldiers.

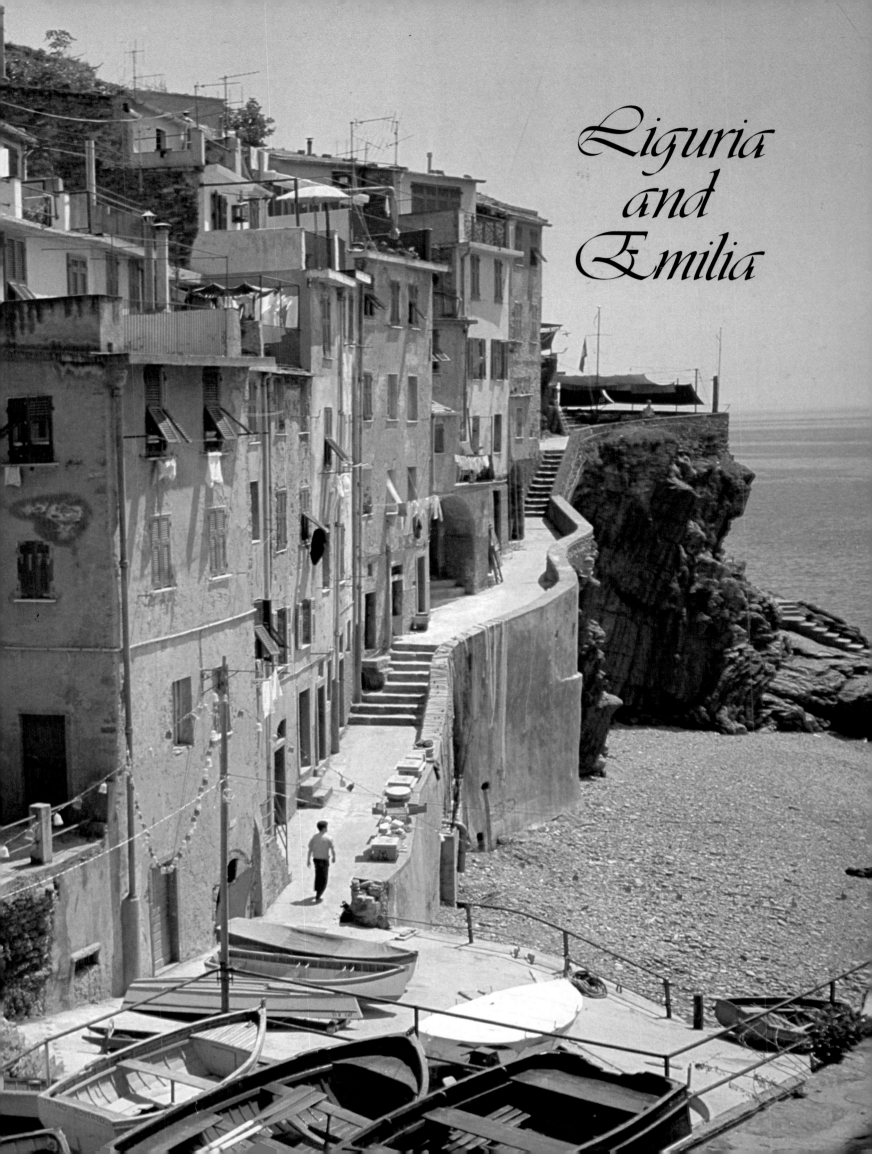

*Liguria
and
Emilia*

Smallest of the Italian provinces, Liguria stretches from the French frontier to the fringes of Tuscany. It lies huddled between the mountains and the sea and has what the guide-books like to call 'a smiling landscape', fertile, diverse and brilliant-hued. The climate is gentle. The succession of soft winters, early springs and long summers transformed the coast and its villages into a string of resorts favoured by Victorian and Edwardian invalids. At San Remo, Edward Lear spent his last years; at Alassio, Elgar composed the overture *In The South*; D. H. Lawrence lived at the little cove of Fiascherino near Lerici; and Max Beerbohm died at Rapallo.

Something of an English sedateness lingers in these towns today. They suggest a life that might include a visit to the library to read the papers from home, a not-too-strenuous game of tennis or croquet, a trundle in a bath-chair along the sea-front, or attendance at Anglican prayers conducted in a hotel parlour by a visiting clergyman. They lack the brashness and chic of their counterparts round the corner in France (Portofino and Santa Margherita are the exceptions) and the unassuming welcome they give to travellers is often more readily appreciated.

The English have gone, but the popularity of places such as Bordighera, Lerici and Sestri Levante is undiminished, thanks largely to the great Italian seaside habit. For many Italians the year inevitably includes a trip to the sea during July and August. Many of the larger houses, once perhaps the villas of individual families, are let out in floors or apartments for the season, and the orderly invasion begins. Elements of British seaside resorts are there – a glut of ice-creams and soft drinks, a tendency to carry a great deal of sand a long way from the beach, and a lot of screaming in the sea – but others are notably lacking. The beaches themselves are cleaner and tidier, the little towns are quieter. The whole experience seems to be better managed, both by the holiday-makers and by those who profit from them.

The people of Liguria are perhaps Italy's most simple and modest. Their way of life, as fishermen and farmers in sheltered villages tucked into the coastal folds below the spurs of the Appennines, has given them a certain bluntness, some might say an enclosed quality. This comes out most strongly in the Genoese. 'The Scots of Italy' they are often called, and their reputation for tight-fistedness and for driving a tough bargain dies hard. There is good historical reason for this, especially among the women. The wives of sailors could never be wholly certain that their husbands would return from their voyaging, and thrift in the face of possible poverty was always exercised.

Genoa itself resists any attempt to define its unique character. It enjoys a beautiful situation matched only by the spectacular loveliness of its former maritime rival, Venice. Rising from its bay to the encircling hills, the city has a defiant grandeur even in its dingier reaches, which amply justifies its title of *La Superba*, the Proud. In its strange fusion of the exotic, the pompous, the squalid and the bizarre it is unlike anywhere else in Italy. Though visited by few travellers the city is always memorable to those who do.

PREVIOUS PAGES *Riomaggiore, one of the Cinque Terre, on the most attractive stretch of the Ligurian coast, makes the perfect beginning to a journey down Italy's western seaboard.*

BELOW *Portofino is rather more obviously a centre for chic pleasure craft. It was especially popular during the 1950s when Italian resorts were visited by millionaires and film personalities. Most of the other ports, harbours and beaches between Genoa and Viareggio are quieter places, noted for their unselfconscious charm and unpolluted seas. Portofino itself lies on a beautiful rocky peninsula dominated by Monte Portofino, and there are many beautiful walks. One delightful fishing village on the peninsula is San Fruttuoso, which lies under Monte Portofino; it is impossible to reach it by car so the only way to get there is by boat or on foot.*

RIGHT *La Spezia, not far along the coast from the Cinque Terre, is on the Gulf of La Spezia. This pleasant town is a trading port and industrial centre. From the promenade there is a view of the Gulf, the Apuan Alps and the nearby marble quarries.*

The pride of Genoa was based firmly on its importance as the dominant seaport of the western Mediterranean during the Middle Ages. Its merchant colonies were planted from the coast of Africa to the shores of the Black Sea. Commercial enterprise enriched the nobles of this independent republic that was ruled by a *doge*. Mercantile competition from Venice and the territorial greed of France, Spain and Austria ultimately helped to dismantle the state. A passionate love of liberty endured here, nevertheless, and Garibaldi's expedition to free Sicily from Bourbon rule in 1860 set sail from Genoa. Still strewn with touches of its earlier dignity in the shape of Baroque palaces and medieval and Renaissance churches, it is the largest port in Italy, with all the attendant bustle, vice and violence. A day in Genoa, taking in as many contrasts as possible, might begin with a visit to the palaces of the Via Garibaldi. This could be followed by a stroll in the old town (left unscathed by wartime bombing), on to the harbour and then the astonishing 19th century cemetery of Staglieno, with its vast galleries of life-size statues – a northern Italian counterpart to the gruesome vault of the Capuchins at Palermo.

As for the sea itself, the stretch of Mediterranean from Nice to La Spezia is now the subject of fierce controversy over pollution and the careless misuse of natural resources. Overfishing has drastically reduced the daily catch and the marine ecology has been disturbed. Otherwise, still safe for swimming in many places, the water remains a placid blue. The richness of its tones is matched in the slow sunsets or in the green of the terraced olives and vines lining the sheer hillsides. Here the soil is among Italy's most fruitful. Something in the combination of air and light and temperature gives whatever grows an extra savour. The juiciest peach tastes sweeter than usual and the famous little yellow mushrooms, the *funghi porcini*, carry a stronger flavour.

Perhaps the most consistently attractive parts of the coast are the Gulf of Spezia and the string of villages known as the Cinque Terre (literally, the Five Lands). The former, almost a kind of marine lake, has special links with the Romantic poets. It was here that Byron stayed for a while at the old fortified outpost of Porto Venere, swimming across to the opposite shore on one occasion to visit Shelley, who lived at Lerici. From Lerici itself in 1822, Shelley and his friend Captain Williams set out on a boat trip, only to be drowned. He was later cremated on an improvised pyre on the beach.

LEFT *Genoa has never lost its sense of grandeur and self-importance as one of Italy's biggest seaports. In 1972 it handled 58 million tonnes of merchandise, the bulk of which consisted of oil and petrol, cereals, cotton, chemicals, and cars. Genoa at one time formed a republic and was known as La Superba, being the main rival of Venice. Rubens and Van Dyck both came here to do portraits of the nobility, many of which are to be found in the city's art galleries. Streets full of opulent palaces are matched by churches in every style from Romanesque to* neo-classical, *and there is some monumental 19th-century building as well. The cathedral, San Lorenzo, dominates the city, which also houses, in the archiepiscopal palace, the* Sacro Catino, *a cup presented by the Queen of Sheba to Solomon, and from which it is believed Christ drank at the Last Supper.*
ABOVE *Just outside the city centre is the massive cemetery of Staglieno. Nowhere is the wealth of the Genoese more evident than in the bizarre display of rows of lifesize marble effigies and sculptured groups in striking attitudes.*

The Cinque Terre are among the most delectable places in southern Europe. All that is lavish and generous in the Mediterranean landscape seems to flourish in abundance here. A walk in the early morning along the cliff-paths linking one village to another presents Liguria at its unmatched best. One major road and the main Genoa – La Spezia railway line link the five towns. The narrow valleys and steep, fertile hillsides make it impossible for any of the little settlements to sprawl too far inland. Few compromises are made for the tourist trade. The red, green and pink-washed housefronts festooned with washing, and the rambling, overhung alleys retain a workaday straightforwardness. The modern quest for the unspoilt or the picturesque is splendidly gratified here. Each town has its hilltop basilicas and chapels, one of which, at Monterosso, contains a Crucifixion by the young Vandyck, who was working in nearby Genoa. Monterosso is also the best vantage point for views along the coast to the other villages such as Vernazza, perched on a jutting headland.

Liguria's inland borders touch those of a province whose character often seems to be typically Italian. Emilia (or to be more precise, Emilia-Romagna) is the name given to the huge, flat river plain of the sluggish Po, which snakes its way across northern Italy to end in a huge marshy delta east of Ferrara. Unlike Britain, France, Germany or the United States, Italy has few fine rivers. The Po, broad and muddy-bordered, is more often a fact to be coped with than an agreeable feature of the landscape. Here those long lines of poplars we saw in Lombardy recur, but the red earth is more fertile. The chequerboard fields between high-banked irrigation ditches alternate with miles of orchards and with the little parks that surround red and yellow farmhouses and arcaded brick barns. This rich soil has given rise to one of the most prosperous farming regions in Europe. It is difficult now to imagine this district as the dreary swamp it was a century ago.

The pig is the monarch of all in Emilia, and variations on the theme are numerous. Bologna gives us the *mortadella*, a cushion-shaped sausage, pale pink and bland to the taste. Parma offers its toothsome *prosciutto*, the crimson ham cut in wafer-thin slices and often served as an appetizer with canteloupe melon. Modena provides, as a winter treat, the succulent *zampone*, a whole pig's trotter of astonishing size.

The Emilian housewife is by tradition the doyenne of cooks in a country which, history suggests, taught kitchen skills even to the French. Besides her cunning with meats and sausages she is adept in preparing various forms of pasta, whether the ribbons of *tagliatelle* and *fettucini*, the plump, stuffed *tortellini* and *ravioli*, or the simple spaghetti. This last is accompanied by a nourishing sauce and sprinkled with the sharp, grated cheese which is another of Parma's delights. To wash everything down there is the light, pink and sparkling Lambrusco wine from Sorbara near Modena.

From the arcades of the Madonna di S. Luca, we look towards the city of Bologna, centre of Italian scholarship, good food and communism. Known to Italians variously as 'The Learned', 'The Fat' and 'The Red', it has all the richly layered life of a dignified and wealthy European city.

Bologna, biggest of Emilia's noble cities, is often called La Grassa, the Fat, and fatness is a symbol of prosperity. Industry as well as agriculture has enriched the province. Not surprisingly, Modena is, per head of population, the wealthiest city in Italy, with Parma not far behind. The people here display an exuberant materialism that often shocks foreign visitors, so completely does it seem to dominate the life of the average Emilian. That almost notorious Italian obsession with *la bella figura*, the look of the thing, which often implies a judgment of the clothes rather than the wearer, or the house as opposed to its owner, is given free rein among the Parmesans and the Modenese. The new car, the new dress, the chic household novelty are all matters of great consequence. Yet this attitude goes hand in hand with a sense of civic pride and responsibility, so that a city like Bologna can take its place among the best-run communities in the modern world.

Bologna has Europe's oldest university, founded in 425 and still at the forefront of scientific research. In the great church of San Petronio, 17th-century musical life saw the birth of the concerto. During the same period the city's patrons of art encouraged the rise of a startlingly original school of painters. Parma nourishes strong musical traditions, and it has been estimated that at least half the orchestral musicians in Italy come from Emilia. As the birthplace of the great conductor Arturo Toscanini it keeps operatic standards ferociously alive in the gorgeous neo-Classical setting of the Teatro Regio.

At nearby Le Roncole is the ramshackle cottage where that most universal of Italian composers, Giuseppe Verdi, was born in 1813. His music never loses touch with the springs of popular feeling and simple melody, and in this directness and spontaneity we find something that belongs peculiarly to Emilia. Modena and Reggio are perhaps the places where this can best be appreciated. They are plain, unpretentious, working cities, though without the dullness or dinginess of northern Europe's industrial towns. In Modena there is a delightful core of old arcaded streets around the massive Romanesque cathedral.

Parma also has its examples of Romanesque. There are the crouching lions of the cathedral porch and the vigorous sculptures with which Benedetto Antelami decorated the octagonal Baptistry, representing the signs of the zodiac and the labours of the months. Romanesque, indeed, is a style found all over the province, whether in the grander basilicas and abbey churches or in the small chapels of country villages.

FAR LEFT *Bologna's main streets are handsomely arcaded; this is a common feature of town centres in the Emilian region. However, Bologna owes its reputation not so much to the delightful, ornate, antique streets as to its pre-eminence in the world of science. It is the home of the famous University of Bologna, founded in 425 AD. Limewood dummies were used there in the 14th century for medical students to practise anatomy; occasionally fresh corpses were used instead. Guglilmo Marconi studied wireless telegraphy there around the turn of this century, and the tradition is upheld today. There are many specialist Institutes and medical and surgical laboratories, and there is also an atomic research centre there.*

LEFT *Parma is well known for its fine buildings. This view shows the Campanile (bell tower) and the octagonal Baptistry designed by Benedetto Antelami in 1196. Antelami was also a talented sculptor, who decorated the interior with groups showing the months and their corresponding zodiac signs. Parma, like many other towns in Italy, had its own style of painting, but it was different in so far as it was a centre for French artists, including the architect Petitot, the sculptor Boudard, and the painter Laurent Pecheux. Parma's other claim to fame comes from the proximity of Colorno, north-east of the city, which was the palace of the Bourbons.*

BELOW *Modena's cathedral belongs to the same period as the Campanile in Parma, and it shows the familiar crouching lions found in the porches of many Romanesque churches. The cathedral itself is dedicated to St Geminian and was designed by the architect Lanfranc. Most of the sculptures were done by Wiligelmo, a 12th-century resident of Lombard. The interior of this magnificent building is constructed of brick and its design is dictated by ogive vaulting. The arches are supported by massive pieces of brickwork and lighter marble piers. The town is renowned today as the home of the Ferrari and the Maserati — both the racing car firms have factories here.*

The Renaissance, however, had its appropriate flowering here in the city of Ferrara, centre of a duchy ruled by the Este family. Related to British royalty (Queen Victoria wanted to change her family name to Este) they combined statecraft, poison, poetry and patronage in the characteristic manner of an Italian princely clan in the 15th and 16th centuries. Here, among the pavilions and palaces, Ludovico Ariosto wrote the poem *Orlando Furioso*, combining epic, fairy-tale and allegory, and named after its mad hero.

Ferrara's mournful quality hints at a failure to reconcile its modern role as a commercial centre with its much more dramatic past. Ravenna is even more grandly desolate, the last vestige in Italy of the old eastern empire of Byzantium. Once a thriving seaport, it became the imperial capital during the turbulent decades of barbarian invasion. It was this period that saw its adornment with a series of churches decorated with dazzling mosaics, representing the finest in Byzantine art of that time. Outstandingly well preserved are those in the tomb of Galla Placidia, sister to the Emperor Honorius, with the scheme of Apostles and Evangelists converging on a central cross.

Poets as well as princesses found a refuge here. Byron found contentment with Countess Guiccioli, his 'last attachment', and Dante, the eternal fugitive, at last gave up his flight in death in 1321. The most refined and consistent of Italian poets, he was able at Ravenna to finish his masterpiece, the trilogy known as *The Divine Comedy*. Its three parts, a journey through Hell and Purgatory leading finally to Paradise and the immortalized Beatrice, were written in Dante's native Tuscan. So was created a form of literary Italian that has endured, in this nation of widely differing dialects, as the language officially used by everyone.

For nearly two centuries Ravenna was in turn capital of the late Roman empire, chief town of the Gothic kings, and seat of the Byzantine governors. This explains the gorgeous mosaic decoration of its churches, considered by many to be the finest in Europe. Outstanding in the story of early Christian art, the brilliantly coloured walls and ceilings of these sturdy basilicas display Biblical scenes and figures from contemporary history.

ABOVE *At San Vitale, Christ as a youthful shepherd feeding his flock crowns the doorway of Galla Placidia's Mausoleum. She was the sister of the emperor Honorius, who fixed his court here in the 5th century. The tomb is thought to be the oldest building in Ravenna, and is notable for the deep, vivid*

blues in its mosaics. It stands next door to the Church of San Vitale which also has a dazzling interior of wonderfully coloured mosaics, mainly in gold, blue and green. Close by are a former monastery of the same name, housing a museum of antiquities, and the tomb of Dante, exiled from Florence, who died in 1321. His tomb lies inside a Classical building of 1780.

RIGHT *The basilica of S. Apollinare in Classe, on the site of an ancient temple of Apollo, 5 km (3 miles) south of Ravenna itself, rather uneasily fuses 6th-century mosaic, featuring Old Testament episodes and church dignitaries of the period, with Baroque fresco. The cylindrical tower dates from the 11th century.*

The Fascination of Tuscany

Even the most hurried of travellers can scarcely fail to notice the presence of the past in Italy. Indeed, it often seems as if there is too much of it to look after. The occasional museum closed for lack of staff, or an art gallery where half the collection is roped off both indicate the difficulty of looking after this vast inheritance for the enjoyment of visitors. For some, Italy is Lancia and Alfa Romeo, for others Gucci and Ferragamo, Alitalia or Olivetti. For a few it is the chance to eat a well-prepared dish of *pappardelle alla lepre* (pasta with hare sauce) washed down with a good bottle of Brunello. But no one can ignore that profound sense of history communicated by the walls, doors, windows and roofs of an Italian city, by its colours and customs, by the very gestures of the people. An acute sense of shape and outline is everywhere to be seen, as is the overall stylishness that makes even the wrapping-up of a box of chocolates

PREVIOUS PAGES *The monastery of S. Antimo, built in 1187, lies near Siena, in the heart of the Tuscan countryside. This is a gentle landscape of rolling hills and fertile valleys planted with vineyards, olives, wheat, maize, mulberries and peppers, in contrast with pine forests and dark cypresses standing against the sky. Solitary Tuscan farmhouses seem to have grown directly out of the soil, so well do they fit into the quiet landscape.*

LEFT *The classic view of Florence is in its rural setting of the hills which rise up from the Arno valley. Brunelleschi's cupola and Giotto's campanile are given pride of place in the city skyline.*

BELOW *The capricious River Arno, memorably disastrous to Florence in the flood of 1966, runs under the Ponte Vecchio, with its dealers in jewellery and fine leatherwork. Along the upper storey of the bridge, which dates from the 14th century, runs a corridor which connects the Uffizi gallery with the Pitti gallery, which houses a famous collection of Raphaels, on the western side of the city.*

ABOVE The charm and surprise of Florence are illustrated by the suddenness with which the city gives way to the country. Peasant vigour mixed with gentleness characterizes Tuscan painting, amply displayed in the galleries of the Uffizi and in the various churches and monasteries which make Florence one of the world's great art centres.

BELOW Tuscan art influenced other Italian schools, most obviously in such pictures as this nativity by the 15th-century Umbrian master Gentile da Fabriano.

RIGHT Florence has all the busy congestion of a mediaeval town. Its narrow streets are lined with tall old houses, with their typical lines of green shutters and sloping eaves. The tourist, resting from the major sights, may stroll along the streets and see everywhere the six-balled shields of the Medicis, the great patrons of the arts in Florence, and other reminders of the constant proximity of masterpieces.

into an artistic flourish. Nowhere better reflects this, over a period of nearly a thousand years, than the province of Tuscany.

A Tuscan, more perhaps than a Roman or a Venetian, will place Italy a firm second in his choice of priorities. Tuscany comes first in everything, and Florence is the flower of all her cities. This flamboyant provincialism has good reasons to support it. For 300 years Tuscany was an independent state, and for almost a decade during the mid-19th century Florence was the capital of a near-united Italy. Tuscany has, what is more, everything it needs for being beautiful, successful and prosperous. Its landscape, now strewn with the renovated homes of expatriate English families, is unparalleled elsewhere in the often tedious countryside of the rest of northern Italy. Its blue-grey olive groves, punctuated with dark green cypresses and rows of brighter-hued vines, cover miles of softly rolling hills. The result is a peculiarly subtle light that is best appreciated in the gradual onset of evenings during spring and early summer.

Its cities, towns, villages and farms maintain the regional tradition of serious hard work. Italy has refused to allow shops and small businesses to be taken over by huge and remote conglomerates. Even if there were such a tendency, the Tuscans for certain would resist it. Enterprises are personally owned and the Tuscans are proud of this and the diligence and application that go with it. The people of Tuscany may seem arrogant and smug, but these traits have grown out of an experience unique in the history of Europe. It was in Tuscany, earlier than in any other part of Italy, that a love of good design and fine workmanship produced an artistic style which formed a brilliant background to the Renaissance. The wealthy merchants of Florence and its neighbouring cities (often fierce commercial and political rivals) were the patrons of painters such as Piero della Francesca, Botticelli, Fra Angelico and Leonardo da Vinci, sculptors like Donatello and Verrocchio, and of that universal genius Michelangelo. All these artists carried the Florentine influence to Rome, Venice, Naples and Milan. Leonardo

spent his last years at the court of France and Michelangelo even received offers of employment from the sultan of Turkey.

The artists of the Italian Renaissance were all solid craftsmen, working for money in shops and business ventures like good Tuscans. A visit to Florence serves to underline this point. There is a softened ruggedness about her great yellow palaces, and town and country meet suddenly on the hillsides above the southern bank of the Arno. Despite appearances, there is here an industriousness that has made Florence one of the busiest and most prosperous cities in Italy. Its great families were merchants. The greatest of them, the Medici, came to power as bankers with commercial links stretching all over Europe.

The last of the Medici, Anna Maria, died in the mid-18th century. She left her huge store of paintings, sculpture, furniture, medals, coins and manuscripts to the city with the proviso that they should not be removed by the Hapsburg dukes who had succeeded to the Tuscan domains. The result is the strong Medici imprint left upon the character of the city. It can be seen in the family coat-of-arms (red balls upon a white ground) over public buildings and in the decoration of numerous places. These include Vasari's frescoes in the crenellated Palazzo Vecchio, Michelangelo's designs for the family tomb in the church of San Lorenzo, and the green marble in the mausoleum of the Medici grand dukes.

And of course there are the paintings themselves. Most are housed in the Uffizi, with its long, airy corridors, and the Pitti, whose rooms are decorated in gilt and brocade with the paintings hung more or less as they were left at the time Medici rule ended. In the Uffizi gallery the early centuries of the Florentine achievement are specially emphasized. There you can see the hollow-eyed saints of Giotto and Masaccio, the delicate work of Botticelli and Ghirlandaio, or the more fanciful styles of Paolo Uccello and Filippino Lippi. The Pitti, on the other hand, displays sumptuous canvasses of the late Renaissance and examples of 16th-century Mannerism. There is also an excellent gallery of 19th-century Italian art.

LEFT The two arms of the Uffizi portico (designed by Giorgio Vasari, in 1560) frame the mediaeval Palazzo Vecchio, ancient seat of government for republican Florentines. The Great Hall on the first floor is thought to contain a lost fresco by Leonardo da Vinci. The Uffizi Museum houses works by Botticelli, Leonardo, Mantegna, Raphael, Michelangelo, Titian, Tintoretto, and many other famous artists, making this one of the finest collections of art in the world.

BELOW Michelangelo's design for the tomb of Guiliano dei Medici, who died in 1516, is part of his magnificent scheme of Medici family monuments for the Sagrestia Nuova at S. Lorenzo, the parish church of the Medicis. Only two of the tombs were actually carried out, though others were certainly intended. The Sagrestia Nuova (New Sacristy) is part of the Medici Chapels within the church, as is the Capella dei Principi (Princes' Chapel), RIGHT, mausoleum of the Medicis, Grand Dukes of Tuscany, in the 17th and 18th centuries. This is an enjoyable example of late Renaissance kitsch. Its dome frescoes, above granite sarcophagi and green marble, are by Pietro Benvenuti and belong to the early 19th century.

Smart, powerful and rich, the city of Dante and Galileo continues to lure the admiring tourist, and Tuscany itself has always provided a haven for English and American expatriates. As we cross the countryside, names like Browning, Lawrence and Forster spring to mind, not only among the olives and cypresses but in the red-roofed towns, none of which is entirely dull. Of them all, Siena is the most self-confidently beautiful. It retains more of an essentially medieval character in the tilt and twist of its narrow streets than Florence has been able to keep. Here there grew up a remarkable school of painters during the Middle Ages, producing what has been aptly called 'a happy art among a happy people' that was tinged with grace and gentleness.

Something of the vibrant strength of the paintings of Duccio, Simone Martini and the Lorenzetti brothers finds an echo in the annual celebration of the Palio, a horse-race run on the sloping oval Campo at the centre of the town. It takes place on 2 July and 16 August each year. Jockeys of the city's 17 wards, drummers and flag-throwers, all in medieval costume, parade before a huge crowd ready to cheer them to victory in the race for the trophy, a banner known as the Palio. The course is a dangerous one, accidents are sometimes fatal, and there are no holds barred. The involvement of the entire city (including a church blessing for the horses) is passionate.

The first of the two races dates from the 17th century, but the second is said to have originated earlier in the celebration of a military victory over the Florentines at Montaperti. Such clashes were frequent in medieval Tuscany and they explain the bristling, defensive look of most of the region's towns. Few places reflect this quality more eloquently than San Gimignano, perched on its hilltop about 18 miles (30 km) to the north of Siena. From a distance it can look suitably grim. Its skyline is punctuated with a clutch of huge towers rising above the high girdle of walls. There were 76 of these towers when Dante came here as ambassador from Florence. Now 13 survive, their greyness softened a little by blotches of green and orange from the houseleeks and wallflowers that grow in their crevices.

The town has a treasure of painting and sculpture, with works by Ghirlandaio and Benedetto da Maiano. In this it is typical of the smaller Tuscan villages and country towns. At Montepulciano, famous for its wines and its yearly music festival, we can admire the elegance of late Renaissance design in streets and squares. At Arezzo, birthplace of the poet Petrarch, we can linger before Piero della Francesca's frescoe sequence *History of the Cross* in the church of San Francesco. Montalcino, last outpost of Sienese independence, still has its 13th-century walls. It contrasts well with the more formal charm of Pienza, enriched in the mid-15th century by Aeneas Silvius Piccolomini, born there and later to become Pope Pius II.

Tuscany is not all art and elegance, however. The countryside changes strikingly from north to south. Nothing offers a more potent contrast with the inland greenness of the Chianti district or the thick woods of Vallombrosa than the bald, stark Maremma plateaux. This district, where malaria was once rife, centres on the gaunt Etruscan city of Volterra. East of Florence as far as the coast, the fertile plain is dotted with nursery gardens. Of its towns Lucca is the most delightfully compact. Here the walls are a noteworthy feature. There is a complete array of late 16th-century ramparts and bastions carrying tree-lined walks and hedging in the dignity of an ancient city-republic which conceded independence only under pressure from Napoleon.

Lucca is especially rich in Romanesque churches. There is one seemingly in every street. Two of the grandest are San Michele in Foro and San Frediano, the latter lying close to the Roman amphitheatre. This amphitheatre is not an exposed ruin such as the Colosseum in Rome itself, but an integral part of the modern city. It is now a vegetable market whose houses and gateways preserve the layout of the ancient circus where gladiators fought. A busy, handsome country town, Lucca is also famous as a centre for the making of olive oil, that staple of the Italian diet.

Tuscany's cooking is as diverse as its land-

scape. It ranges from the thick Florentine beefsteak to the fish dishes of Livorno, the region's biggest seaport. There are wild boar, tripe and artichokes to enrich the table as well. In a country where cakes and puddings tend to be dull or merely unnecessary, there is a surprising wealth of sweet things here. They include the dark chestnut cake known as *Castagnaccio*, tempting Sienese macaroons or, from the same town, the sweet and sticky *Panforte*, which is made of nuts, candied fruit, almonds and cloves.

In case digestion proves a problem there is always a spa or two nearby. Those at Montecatini, Chianciano and Bagni di Lucca are some of the best. The spa habit still thrives in Italy, and these little watering places, with their seasonal clientele and state-run thermal establishments, make an interesting feature of the region. Especially attractive is Bagni di Lucca, which lines the hillsides in the chestnut-hung valleys of the fast-flowing Lima and Serchio rivers. Bagni, as it is often called, has always had a particular attraction for English people with its mild climate, dense woodlands and sedate village atmosphere. It comes as no surprise to find, in this spot once visited by Shelley and the Brownings, a little Anglican cemetery among the chestnut groves by the river. It is a romantic memorial to Victorian invalids and exiles.

BELOW LEFT Siena lies around the mouth of a natural crater, encircled by ramparts. The hills on which it is built are red clay from which the colour burnt siena is named. Thought to have been founded at the beginning of the Roman era, Siena became a free republic in the Middle Ages and thrived as a trade centre.
LEFT In the centre of the crater is the huge Piazza del Campo, which is shaped like a fan. Eleven streets lead into this square, which is dominated by the Palazzo Pubblico (town hall), symbol of the city's former independence and one of the finest public buildings in Italy. Its graceful Gothic structure (1288–1309) is outlined in shadow in the picture, which gives an idea of the height of the tower, the Torre del Mangia which, at 88m (286½ ft) high, offers superb views from its summit.
BELOW The Campo is the scene of the twice-yearly Palio, the 'Palio delle Contrade', to give it its full name. This, the most popular festival in Siena, is the exciting horse race to which the competing jockeys are escorted by members of their contrade (wards) in 15th-century costume. Bands play, flags fly, and the race is fast, furious and tough. The contrade are named after beasts, reptiles and birds, and the prize is an embroidered palio (banner), inscribed with the coat of arms of the town.

Pisa was another favourite with wanderers, though nowadays it is a rather forlorn place that lacks much of the grandeur and theatrical self-confidence of towns such as Siena or Lucca. Everyone knows Pisa, however, for its leaning tower. It is the dominant feature of a striking ensemble of cathedral, baptistry and cemetery. These revive the glories of an age when Pisa, at the mouth of the Arno, was a maritime republic that challenged Genoa and Venice for supremacy in the Mediterranean. With her merchant spoils she built the black and white marble cathedral and raised the nearby campanile which, while it was still in the making, began to lean out of true. It now tilts at a rate of about 2·8 mm (1/10 in) every four years.

With such a profusion of good things, both natural and man-made, from the snow slopes of Abetone to the textile mills of Prato and the altar of a simple village church such as Carmignano's, it is not surprising that Tuscany should feel just a little pleased with itself. If ever a region so freely displayed everything that Italy has given to the civilized world, it is surely found here.

BELOW *Pisa has a curious atmosphere: that of a deserted capital city. It was once a busy commercial port and the grand centre of the Pisan republic. Everyone knows the Leaning Tower of Pisa, but less familiar are the delicate Romanesque Duomo and the Baptistry, which is Romanesque with Gothic additions, with which it forms an ensemble. Begun in 1174, the tower gained its famous tilt soon afterwards; this increases slightly every year. Here the astronomer and physicist Galileo (1564–1642) made his experiment with lead and feathers to determine gravitational laws. All three buildings are of marble, and the Cathedral has a particularly beautiful pulpit. The dome of the Baptistry is 35 m (115 ft) in diameter.*

LEFT *San Gimignano's frowning towers still suggest the nervous, aggressive face of a town which played a key rôle in the power struggles of mediaeval Tuscany. Originally 72 in number, there are now 14 of these towers, which were built in the 14th century by noble families for use as keeps. Each family built its tower as high as possible, for reasons of prestige.*

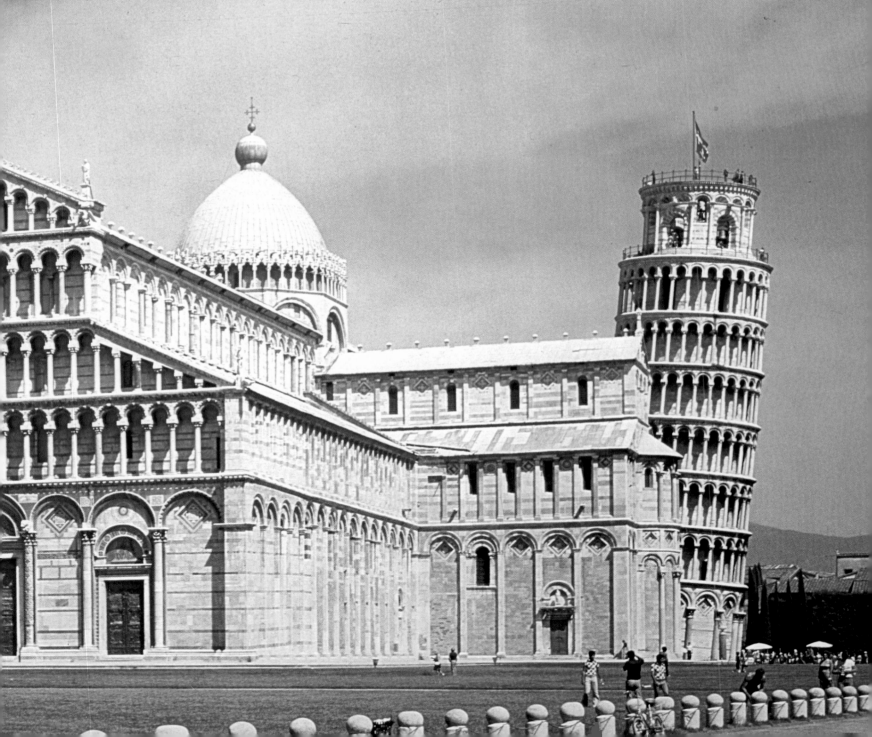

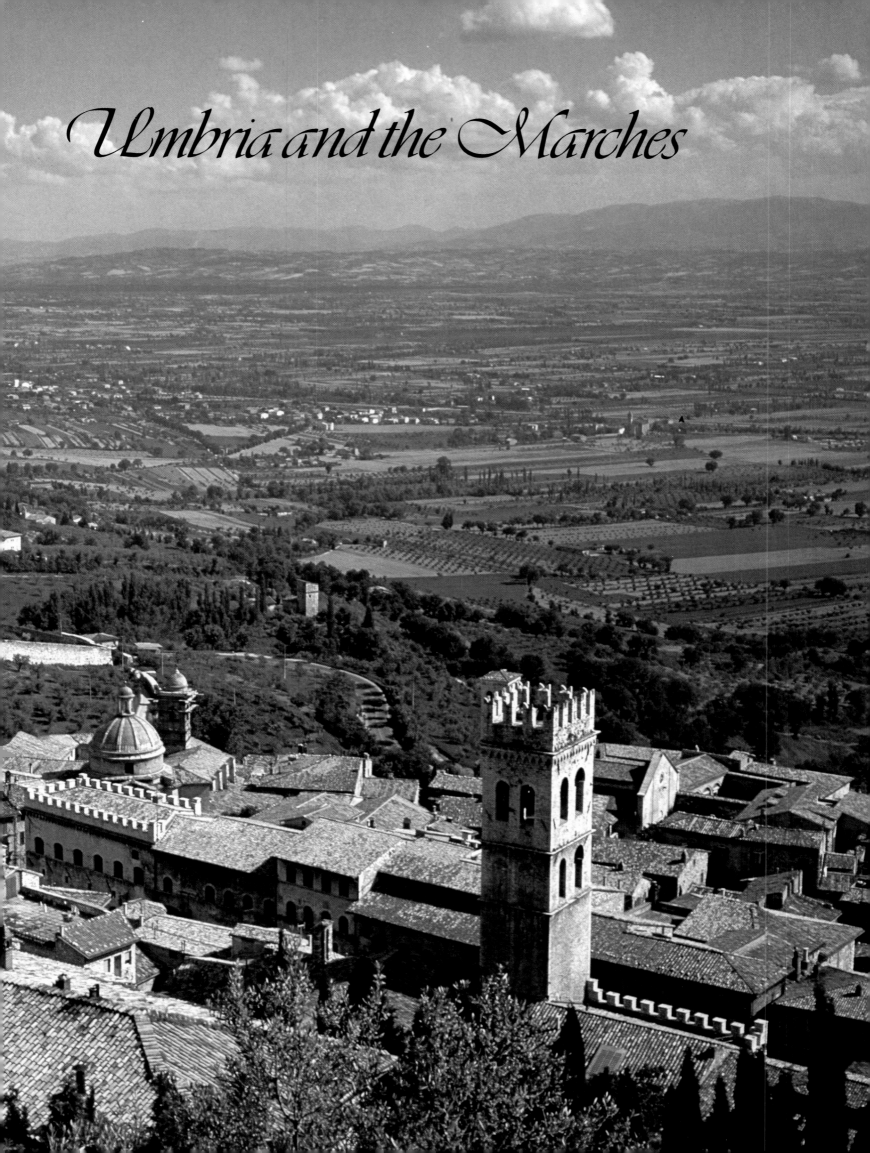

Umbria and the Marches

In a country as devout as Italy it comes as no surprise to find a wealth of Christian saints. In Lombardy we recall St Charles Borromeo and St Ambrose, the learned and forceful bishop of Milan. Venice preserves the relics of St Mark and St Lucy, which were carried off by merchant venturers. Tuscany has its own array of martyrs, bishops and hermits. These include St Catherine of Siena and the child saint Fina de' Ciardi, the nobleman's daughter from San Gimignano whom St Gregory summoned to join him in Paradise. But no region seems richer in saintliness than Umbria, the hilly, wooded heartland of Italy.

Looking at the intensively farmed Italian landscape, where the farm animals are kept in sheds and every available piece of ground is cultivated, we may find it hard to imagine the country as it looked in the remote past. Umbria comes nearest of all to offering us a glimpse of an older Italy. It thus seems to provide an ideal atmosphere for prayer and contemplation. There is, too, the ghostly presence of the ancient Umbrians and Etruscans. Etruscan art concentrated primarily on sculpture and fresco painting to commemorate the dead, and the territory between Florence and Rome is marked with the remains of tombs.

Though they eventually conquered them, the Romans respected the Etruscans for their profound religious observance. It is said that even at the fall of the city of Rome to the Goths in the early Christian era, soothsayers of Etruscan descent were called upon to consult the omens. At more or less the same period, in the town of Norcia between Terni and Spoleto, twins were born whose efforts would prolong this ancient religious tradition into the Christian world. St Benedict and his sister St Scholastica are among the great names in the story of the Church during the so-called Dark Ages of Western civilization.

Practically every place in Umbria seems to hold some sacred association or other. About 4 miles (6 km) away from Norcia lies Cascia, home of St Rita, patron of all those who pray for something impossible to happen. She is, as a result, a highly popular saint. Among many other devout Umbrian women who sought to follow the religious life were St Angela of Foligno and St Clare of Assisi, founder of the Order of Poor Clares. At Todi, lovers of Christian poetry will remember the *Stabat Mater*, the fine Latin sequence on the Crucifixion composed here in the late 13th century by the mystic Iacopone.

Centre of any Umbrian pilgrimage, however, is the romantically sited town of Assisi. It is on the edge of Monte Subasio, south-east of Perugia. Here in 1182 Francesco Bernardone, better known as St Francis, was born into a rich merchant's family. After a reckless youth and service as a soldier he turned to the work of God, giving away worldly possessions and befriending beggars and lepers. His example prompted others to form a little community around his chapel on Monte Subasio. In 1209 the Pope sanctioned Francis's rule of chastity, poverty and obedience. The reputation of Francis carried him beyond Assisi to other parts of Italy, to Spain and even to Egypt, where he was allowed to preach before

the sultan. Two years before his death he received on his body the stigmata or wounds of Christ, and in 1228 he was canonized.

Remembered above all as the saint of the poor and the needy and the friend of birds and animals, whom he called his 'brothers and sisters,' he is a vivid presence in Assisi today. The two-storeyed Basilica di San Francesco commemorates him most notably in the fresco panels above the high altar ascribed to Giotto. The same artist also portrayed marvellously a series of episodes from the saint's career on the walls of the upper church. Other artists, including Cimabue and Simone Martini, helped embellish the Basilica. Even for those with no religious feelings the twin churches form an astonishing textbook of Italian medieval art at its purest.

In the cathedral we are shown the font where St Francis and his follower St Clare were baptized. San Damiano preserves the scene of the saint's renunciation of the world, and the church of Sta Maria degli Angeli holds the oratory of the Porziuncola, where the Franciscan brothers first gathered.

PREVIOUS PAGES *Assisi, spread out in the soft Umbrian light on the slopes of Monte Subasio, commands breathtaking views of the rolling, fertile countryside. The town has hardly changed since mediaeval times. Home of St Francis, who preached kindness to animals, Assisi is a centre of religious art which developed under his influence and that of his contemporary, St Clara, who founded the Order of the Poor Clares.*

ABOVE *The rose window and pointed arches of the doorway indicate that Assisi's Upper Church was built in the mid-13th century. The Lower Church, immediately beneath it, was begun in 1228 by Jacopo Tedesco. Rich frescoes adorn both churches: in the upper church those depicting the life of St Francis were painted by Giotto between 1296 and 1304. The tall and graceful nave is light and airy, in contrast with the darkness and low construction of the lower church.*

LEFT *The groined vaults of the lower church's sanctuary frame paintings by Giotto, illustrating the essential Franciscan vows: towards the nave, the saint's marriage with Poverty is depicted; towards the south transept, Chastity is personified; towards the north transept, Obedience is shown. Towards the apse is illustrated the Triumph of St Francis. There are many other frescoes in the lower church, and the tomb of St Francis, not discovered until 1818, is in the crypt.*

BELOW *True Tuscan warmth and spontaneity characterize Giotto's treatment of the Nativity. Angels hail Mary and the Christ Child and summon the shepherds to Bethlehem, while friends wash and swaddle the baby. Giotto revolutionized painting by introducing naturalism and emotion into his work, discarding Byzantine-style decoration for simplicity, and emphasizing the spiritual meaning of the scenes he painted.*

Grander, though inevitably less sacred a spot than Assisi, is Perugia. It hangs above the river Tiber that snakes its way among the hills down to Rome, and has an air of studious calm as befits its role as one of Italy's senior university towns. Besides the university itself, housed in a former monastery but originally founded in 1307, Perugia possesses a well-known department of Italian studies for foreign students.

The old Etruscan city of Perugia, whose traces can still be seen in the city's defences, was destroyed in a Roman siege and rebuilt by the Emperor Augustus. Its medieval history follows the usual Italian pattern of stern despots and rival families, but this turbulent period also produced a magnificent school of painters. Chief among these, during the 15th century, were the two masters nicknamed Il Perugino and Il Pinturicchio. Their delicately romantic interpretations of religious themes form the centrepieces of the collection of Umbrian art in Perugia's Galleria Nazionale.

More fine paintings may be found in the city's churches, such as San Pietro dei Cassinensi and the cathedral, and students of architecture find much to enjoy here as well. It often seems as though Perugia's citizens managed to assemble the choicest examples of work of individual designers. Few of the major buildings of the town are without some touch of distinction. Visitors especially admire the Collegio del Cambio, the grand frescoed guildhall of the bankers, where Perugino mingled Christian and pagan elements in a typically Renaissance manner. The lofty Palazzo dei Priori, twice rebuilt in the Middle Ages, carries an outside staircase and a pulpit used for public addresses by civic dignitaries. The griffin and the lion above the doorway on this side of the palace represent Perugia

herself and the Guelph (Papal) party she supported. The chains they carry are those of the city gates of Siena, carried off in a raid in 1358.

Every traveller to Perugia remembers the Fontana Maggiore, that handsome ensemble of bronze and marble in the Piazza Quattro Novembre. It was created in the 13th century by Fra Berignate and the sculptors Nicola and Giovanni Pisano. The square itself, which surrounds the central fountain with the grim beauties of a string of medieval palaces, is one of the great examples of that important Italian concept, the open piazza. At the heart of any town, large or small, the piazza has always offered a ready theatre for the dramatic events of a community's history. This has been so whether in medieval riots, demonstrations during the Risorgimento, Italy's bid for national unity, or in modern rabble-rousing by 20th-century demagogues. It will, of course, also serve as an admirable meeting place, for a stroll, a drink in a bar or a café, or for one of those long, gesture-punctuated conversations that are a feature of the Italian city scene. The Piazza Quattro Novembre at Perugia thus forms a worthy counterpart to other great open spaces such as Milan's Piazza del Duomo, Venice's Piazza San Marco or the Piazza della Signoria in Florence.

Two other places of exceptional interest are Gubbio and Spoleto. If there is any spot which typifies the Italian scene at its most picturesque, then Gubbio is surely it. Associations with St Francis are various. They include the delightful story of the wolf which, after terrorizing the local countryside, was miraculously tamed by the saint and, as 'brother wolf,' became the pet of Gubbio's inhabitants. The town is also famous for its brightly glazed pottery known as majolica. This comes in

ABOVE The Piazza 4 Novembre, in the heart of the mediaeval town of Perugia, is one of the most attractive squares in Italy with its great fountain, cathedral and the tremendous Palazzo dei Priori (Prior's Palace). This palace, shown above, was begun in 1281 and remodelled in 1333, and represents the finest flowering of Italian Gothic design. Its emphasis on combining civic grandeur with fortress-like defensiveness is typical of an independent city state of the Middle Ages. The staircase leads up to a pink and white marble pulpit from which the priors preached. The bronze griffin over the doorway is Perugia's own symbol.

RIGHT Similar in its intention to the Palazzo dei Priori is the Ducal Palace at Urbino, built a century and a half later. It cleverly unites Gothic design with the new Renaissance ideas, and the striking mass of its walls and towers was much admired by contemporaries. Smaller imitations of it can be found all over eastern Italy. Urbino itself is a peaceful city of steep and narrow streets, once an independent duchy ruled by the Montefeltro family who were great patrons of the arts during the 15th century. Urbino was finally handed over to the Church in 1626, when Pope Urban VIII persuaded the last duke to abdicate.

colours that are mainly blue, green, yellow and orange. The winding streets of red-roofed houses converge on the imposing Piazza della Signoria, where the Palazzo dei Consoli, begun in 1332 by Matteo di Giovanello, is a great moment of medieval design. Inside, the museum displays the fascinating Eugubian Tables, a series of priestly laws that date from the 2nd century BC. These are written in three languages, Etruscan, Umbrian and Latin.

ABOVE *The pilgrimage church of Santa Maria della Consolazione at Todi has a fine Renaissance completeness. Built in the form of a Greek cross and full of a soaring grace and strength, it is the work of Cola di Matteuccio da Caprarola (1508), advised by Baldassare Peruzzi. It was not completed until 1604, and may, very indirectly, have helped to inspire some of Sir Christopher Wren's designs for St Paul's Cathedral in London. The church is just outside Todi itself, an attractive old town with three sets of walls still preserved: the Etruscan, the Roman and the mediaeval. The town is beautifully situated in the softly rounded hills of the Umbrian landscape.*

ABOVE RIGHT *White oxen draw the plough in a typical Umbrian landscape of rolling fields and hills, which retains the character it had in ancient times more than any other part of rural Italy. Birthplace of many Christian saints, Umbria has an atmosphere which seems ideal for prayer, contemplation, and the life of the mystic. Italy's mountainous spine and generally stony terrain means that every available space is cultivated and there is little grazing except for sheep. Cows are kept at the farm and much milk and beef is imported.*

Spoleto is another of the older Umbrian cities whose character has been comparatively unscathed by social and political change. The biggest innovation in the town's recent life has been the yearly Festival of Two Worlds organized by the composer Giancarlo Menotti. This takes place all over the town. Like the Montepulciano festival in Tuscany, it seeks to involve the local people in its activities. There are two beautiful old theatres here, as well as the remains of a Roman amphitheatre. The town is superbly contained within its walls. These, like the aqueduct of the Ponte delle Torri crossing the river Tessino, rest on Roman foundations.

We remember the Romans also at the nearby springs of Clitumnus, clear and osier-fringed. These inspired poets like Virgil and Byron, though painters touring Umbria tended to be more enthusiastic over the Cascata delle Marmore near Terni, south of Spoleto. These falls, nowadays harnessed for industrial use, are man-made Roman works that were intended to prevent flooding by throwing one river over a precipice into another. Umbria is, in fact, one of the more watery reaches of Italy. Between Perugia and Orvieto lies the broad lake of Trasimeno. Scene of Hannibal's defeat of Quintus Fabius in 217 BC, it is slowly drying into an expanse of peat. There is still enough of it, however, to arrest the traveller

who is in search of romantic seclusion.

Orvieto belongs officially to Tuscany, but in every other sense it is purely Umbrian. No one can remain unmoved by its amazing Duomo, a composition of marble and mosaic with echoes in other Italian cathedrals but surely unrivalled anywhere for sheer flamboyance. The façade demands to be read rather than merely looked at. There are Biblical stories on the pilasters, a series of restored mosaics, and eloquent sculpture by Andrea Pisano, as well as modern doors of bronze. Apart from the fresco work by local artists Ugolino del Prete and Gentile da Fabriano, there is inside the additional wonder of the Cappella Nuova, decorated by Fra Angelico and Luca Signorelli. No two painters could have been more divergent in style. Yet Signorelli was in his late teens by the time Fra Angelico died, and he merely completed in 1504 what his predecessor had left unfinished 50 years earlier.

The spread of Renaissance culture throughout Italy is nowhere better appreciated than in the Marche, east of Umbria. The Marche comprise three 'marches' or provinces. The whole region is one of the least known to the tourist. This may be because of the relatively rough and hilly terrain, or simply because, apart from Venice, Italy's larger centres tend to lie west of the Apennines.

There is much to see and enjoy in this area. Travellers arriving by sea from Greece or Yugoslavia are likely to know Ancona, one of Italy's largest ports. It has stood up well to sieges, bombardments and natural disasters. Contact with Dalmatia meant that architects such as Giorgio da Sebenico (Juraj Dalmatinac, from Sibenik across the Adriatic) could flourish here in the 15th century. The city also nourished that bizarre Renaissance figure, Cyriac of Ancona, whose career as a merchant trading to Greek ports enabled him to import Greek culture into Italy with cargoes of manuscripts. He kept lively journals, restored some of the local Roman monuments and was a visitor to the Turkish sultan at the time of the fall of Constantinople.

The most famous writer of the Marche was a far sadder figure.This was the 19th-century poet Giacomo Leopardi. He led a sheltered life before going to Rome and Naples and an early death. His poems, full of romantic pessimism and frustration, have become world famous. Something of this mood can perhaps be traced to his ancestral Palazzo Leopardi in the little town of Recanati, scene of his childhood. Happier places on this eastern edge of Italy are Pesaro and Fano. The former was the birthplace of one of the world's best-loved composers, Gioacchino Rossini, whose overtures set feet tapping with their lively rhythms

and witty orchestration. Rossini, 'the Swan of Pesaro,' was the master of comedy in music. Operas such as *The Barber of Seville* and *La Cenerentola* made him a celebrity in Naples before Paris claimed him as the father of grand opera with *William Tell*.

Inland from Fano, with its memories of the powerful Malatesta family, lies Urbino, a sort of eastern outpost of the Tuscan Renaissance. The city commands instant respect from its spectacular position, and the focus of any visit will be its colossal Palazzo Ducale. Typically of many buildings in the Marche, its architect, Luciano Laurana, was a Dalmatian who used pale limestone from his native country. The powerful Duke Federico da Montefeltro was the guiding spirit behind this. He was also responsible for the creation of the famous 'Studio' in the palace that features inlay work by Botticelli. Federico patronized painters such as Piero della Francesca and Paolo Uccello, some of whose canvases can be seen here. Also noteworthy are the stark, vivid frescoes by the Salimbeni brothers in the Oratorio di San Giovanni. But Urbino is most famous as the home town of Raffaello Sanzio, known to the world as Raphael. Born here in 1483, Raphael's unique talent was encouraged in Tuscany but flowered most obviously in works such as the grand *Stanza* or Rooms of the Vatican Museums in Rome.

The
Majesty of Rome

Like so many clichés, the assertion that all roads lead to Rome contains a grain or two of truth. Rome symbolizes two types of power, the worldly and the religious. These two powers fought each other for a time, combined for a while, then split apart, leaving the city as the centre of the Christian world. Yet though her empire was destroyed, Rome's significance was permanently established. Europe, Africa and the Middle East are criss-crossed with her roads and pitted and hummocked with the ruins of her colonial cities. Roman merchants travelled to the wilds of central Asia and as far east as the Mekong Delta. The Western world has inherited some of her laws and institutions, and the English language is heavily laden with Latin derivations.

Christian peoples regard Rome either as a spiritual guide, a benevolent friend or an ever-present threat. In whatever guise, the city — capital of one of the world's most influential religions — acts as both a focus and a symbol. Under papal rule it was the chief city of an independent territory. The popes were thus temporal as well as spiritual rulers. Even today, in an official sense, they are political leaders at the head of the world's smallest state. The Vatican City produces its own stamps and coins, and has its own radio station and printing presses. It exercises special rights over some of the larger Roman churches as well. For papal security four guard corps are on hand. These are the famous Swiss Guard in their Renaissance uniform, reputedly designed by Michelangelo, the Palatine Guard with plumed helmets, the Noble Guard and the Pontifical Police.

It would be foolish to pretend that all the popes throughout history were perfectly adapted to their great responsibility of office. Some of them were career churchmen with an eye to worldly advantage. Others were shrewd politicians, using religion as a weapon of statecraft. Others again were scholarly dreamers ill-suited to dealing with the variety of problems that have always confronted the Roman Catholic Church. And some were simply men from the right social background, whom the cardinals and their aristocratic relatives found acceptable. But many of the popes have been men of vision and authority, setting an example to the millions of faithful under their care. As proof that this leadership has never lost its appeal, we have only to see the vast crowds that gather in St Peter's Square every Easter Day to receive the apostolic blessing. Few sights are more moving, or do more to underline the continuing need felt by Christians for a sense of spiritual direction.

Rome's other major role belongs very much to the immediate moment. The city is, of course, the capital of a modern republic. It is thus the centre of Italy's government and the hub of her wild and complex political life. Italian politics are barely comprehensible even to those who read the papers and follow events closely. Yet politics is a mania among Italians. National enthusiasm for making everything, from education to opera, into a burning political issue, may be traced to the fact that until the fall of Mussolini in 1943 Italy had no political life worth mentioning. It needs to be remembered that only in 1946 did the monarchy formally give way to an elective republic. Italy's present electoral system is calculated to produce a constant tussle between governors and governed. As one party after another fails to find quite the right balance or compromise to create a majority coalition in Parliament, the Italians watch the shifting scene with fascination.

PREVIOUS PAGES The weed-grown ruins of the Roman Forum have their own special poetic melancholy. Once the civil, commercial and religious centre of Ancient Rome, abandoned after the Barbarian invasion in the 5th century AD, these fragments of temples and palaces still testify to the once mighty empire. The Colosseum can be seen in the background.
ABOVE St Peter's Square, Rome, by Bernini, makes a spectacular setting for the church of St Peter's itself. Built in 1667, the colonnades, with room for two carriages abreast and topped by statues of saints, underline the theatrical quality of an Italian piazza. The colonnade is generally regarded as Bernini's greatest architectural achievement. The principal function of the huge area was to contain the enormous crowds that gathered for the papal benediction at Easter and on other religious occasions. The need for a penetrable enclosure was answered by the construction of the colonnades. In the centre of the piazza is the Vatican obelisk which was placed there by Sixtus V in 1586. Bernini moved a fountain by the architect Carlo Maderno into the long axis of the piazza and then built a replica on the other side.
RIGHT The awe and majesty of the Church as the guardian of Christianity are the very points which Renaissance popes wished to emphasize. Here in the Sistine Chapel Michelangelo created the classic statement of these ideas in his ceiling frescoes, begun in 1508 and taking four years to complete. Here the fully developed curves and cornices of pagan classicism are harnessed to the story of the Creation and Fall of Man. The predominant mood of this work is of harmony which contrasts markedly with his painting of The Last Judgment on the wall behind the altar, which is imbued with an atmosphere of a fear-ridden, anxious, brooding humanity.

RIGHT The Scala di Spagna, the Spanish Steps, created in 1721, form one of Rome's most extravagant architectural gestures. Although their name suggests they owe their presence and form to the Spanish, they are really French in conception. They were suggested by the French at a time when the Spanish Embassy was being built in the 17th century and they were paid for with a legacy from a French diplomat. At the head of the Steps, from which there is a magnificent view, is the French-built church and convent of Trinita dei Monti, which was constructed in 1495 following a donation from the French king, Charles VIII. The Steps, lined with flower stalls, rise from the Piazza di Spagna (which has a 17th-century boat-shaped fountain) at the centre of the former 'Strangers Quarter' in Rome where foreign visitors in past times used to stay. Charles Dickens described the Steps as being peopled with unemployed artists' models, and they remain today as a place to loiter or meet friends, for students and visitors alike. Part of the attraction of the Steps lay in the nature of the area – it was filled with artists' studios and galleries. In 1821 the romantic poet, John Keats, died in a house on the Steps, and this has now been made into a museum. The area today is less Bohemian than it used to be and has been taken over by more exclusive shops and restaurants.

LEFT Equally attractive to poets, painters and composers, were the cascades and fountains of Tivoli, in the gardens of the Villa d'Este, about 30 km (19 miles) from Rome. From the terraced gardens, down which the water tumbles, there is a succession of beautiful views of the Roman Campagna.

On a more sinister level, political life has become linked with the age-old Italian problem of what is and is not corrupt. Is it right for a man with influence to use that power for giving other members of his family a helping hand? Should a party boss also be a patron? Where do the Church, the Mafia and big business play their part? Now and then these questions are aired when a scandal bursts in the newspapers.

Rome naturally provides a focus for the Italian press, radio and television. Until a few years ago it was also one of the world's great film centres. The studios of Cinecittà produced everything from super-epic to situation comedy, and fashionable stars and directors visited the city if only to be seen there. Rome has also created its own form of style, quite distinct from anything to be found in Paris, London or New York. The main shopping streets display wares of unrivalled elegance, and deliberate appeal is made to that special Italian feeling for colour and line.

Sometimes, under the sheer weight of tourism, it is difficult to find the modern area of Rome, where its citizens live. But it is there, vigorous and real. The Romans have a reputation elsewhere in Italy for complacent laziness. Among Italian communities abroad, where you find Neapolitans, Sicilians, Emilians and Piedmontese you are unlikely to find many Romans. Their attitude towards the city they love is summed up in the famous cry of the stagecoach drivers as St Peter's came into view. 'Ecco Roma!' they would call to the passengers, with a grand gesture and maybe a shrug of the shoulders to follow, 'That's Rome!' Unspoken, but implied, were the words 'take it or leave it'.

The Romans often seem to have the most strongly marked character of any of the peoples of Italy. They are pleasure-loving, somewhat lackadaisical, rather eccentric and perhaps a little uninterested in the world beyond. Their thick local accent is easily noticed, though not so easily understood by outsiders.

Few things are more enjoyable in Rome than a long lunch in one of the many excellent restaurants. Some of the best are close to the Pantheon and the Campo dei Fiori in the oldest part of the city. Others are to be found in Trastevere, once the poorest quarter but now fashionable among the host of expatriate writers and artists always to be seen in Rome. Everything is good to eat, from the pasta to the various kinds of local cake and confectionery. But one of the really memorable items of any Roman meal is the salad. This is never a solitary wad of pallid lettuce leaves – instead, a succulent bouquet of different sorts of edible grass, dandelion and greenstuff, both bitter and sweet.

Rome is a city of beautiful structures. It was made in three distinct periods. Of the city of the Tarquins, the Republic and the Caesars, up until the 3rd century AD, we can see such tremendous monuments as the Colosseum, the Arch of Constantine and the Baths of Caracalla. The historic Forum preserves the nucleus of everything sacred to the Romans of the past. Its open plan, a grouping of major civic and religious buildings, was copied in imperial towns from Britain to Turkey. It is the direct ancestor of every Italian piazza.

On top of this the Renaissance popes, a succession of warriors, politicians and art patrons laid the fabric of a new city from the 15th century. In the dignity and lofty magnificence of their building they sought to reinterpret the spirit of the ruins among which they lived. After 1,000 years a spirit of pomp and splendour returned to Rome. Architects looked at structures such as the Pantheon, surviving from the reign of Augustus in the 1st century BC, and learned from them. In the enormous tepidarium or luke-warm room of the Baths of Diocletian, Michelangelo actually created the church of Santa Maria degli Angeli.

The third great moment in the making of modern Rome came at the beginning of the 17th century. The papacy by then was something to be handed round among the great families of the city, all of which had members who were cardinals. They may have been unworthy of the papacy but they were rich patrons of art and architecture. To this period belong the broad squares such as the Piazza Navona, parks and gardens like those of the Villa Borghese, and churches such as Borromini's exquisite San Carlo alle Quattro Fontane. This was the opulent Rome of the artist Caravaggio and, later, of the exiled Queen Christina of Sweden. The only truly great painter of 17th-century Italy, Caravaggio came to Rome from northern Lombardy. It was in Rome that he produced a series of religious paintings notable for their intensely dramatic use of light. His wild, bohemian career ended in a knife-fight over the score in a tennis match, and he died of a fever at the age of only 37.

Sometimes in the blending of Baroque, Renaissance and antique, it appears as if Rome has sprung up organically like some maturing natural substance. The subtle hues of red and brown in the stone, the sudden dashes of yellow, the darkened tones of some ancient marble – all these blur into a harmony of styles and forms. Now and then we find actual fragments of a Roman temple incorporated in a church, and its columns used again to create a nave and aisles. But this is all very much the work of man, and in case we forget there are the strong imprints of Michelangelo and Bernini to remind us.

The sympathy these two artists had for their historic surroundings made them the greatest individual creators of present-day Rome. Besides completing the dome of St Peter's and decorating the Sistine Chapel, Michelangelo also planned the glorious Piazza del Campidoglio, centred on the equestrian statue of Marcus Aurelius. His hand as a sculptor can be seen in the frowning figure of Moses, which was created for the mausoleum of his master, Julius II, in the Basilica of San Pietro in Vincoli.

Bernini belongs to a generation that immediately followed Michelangelo's. Like the earlier artist he was both sculptor and architect and used these gifts to enrich Baroque Rome with fountains, statues and squares. Bernini created the enormous arcaded arms of St Peter's Square and the voluptuous curves of statuary in the Fountain of the Four Rivers in the Piazza Navona. Bernini is at his most memorable as a sculptor. Visitors who find other aspects of the Roman Baroque too ugly or grotesque are always prepared to acknowledge Bernini's mastery of the materials he worked with. St Peter's has the exciting *Vision of Constantine* and elsewhere in the city his feeling for drama and sensation can be seen in works such as *St Teresa in Ecstacy* or *Apollo and Daphne*.

The Fountain of the Four Rivers is just one of countless fountains that give character to Rome's open spaces. The city has become famous, too, for its parks and gardens. Once there were many more trees and the climate was more favourable to winter and summer visitors. But even now a stroll on the Pincio above the city or in the gardens of the Villa Medici on a spring or autumn afternoon imparts an essentially Roman delight.

From certain of these places along the hills on which Rome lies we can look across the city towards the countryside beyond. This has always been one of Italy's most attractive parts, and wealthy Romans have favoured its towns as summer resorts. The area on the south-east edge of Rome, known as the Castelli Romani, has remained popular since ancient times. The orator Cicero, for example, kept a villa at Tusculum. Later, in the nearby town of Frascati, Prince Charles Edward Stuart, 'Bonnie Prince Charlie', ended an eventful if disappointing life of attempts to win back the throne of England.

ABOVE *Rome of the Kings, the Republic and the Caesars has only been laid bare in comparatively recent times. (For centuries the Forum's overgrown ruins were a pasture for cattle.) The Colosseum, however, has always symbolized for the world the splendour, ambition and cruelty of imperial Rome. Opened in 80 AD by the Emperor Vespasian, its vast oval contained seating for 50,000 spectators at gladiatorial combats and wildbeast shows. A warren of cellars underneath the arena sheltered the animals* *themselves, the gladiators and their trainers, and (by tradition) the various Christian martyrs who perished for their faith here by being thrown to the lions. The outside of the building is formed of the Doric, Ionic and Corinthian orders, one above the other. 'While the Colosseum stands,' said an ancient prophecy, 'Rome shall stand; when the Colosseum falls, Rome shall fall; when Rome falls, the world shall fall'.*

Like the other towns in these Alban Hills, Frascati is full of patrician villas and palaces. All of them have majestic sweeps of garden, with fountains and terraces. It is here that we meet again those two typical garden trees, the cypress and the ilex, which give the fundamentally Italian look to the landscape of Tuscany and Umbria. An additional charm is given to the Castelli district by the two lakes of Nemi and Albano. The mysterious green tinge of Nemi enhances its fame as the sacred pool of the goddess Diana, whose cult was celebrated in the nearby grove. On the shores of Albano lies the Albano Laziale, which brings us close to the earliest springs of Roman culture. For this is traditionally the town of Alba Longa, founded in 1150 BC by Ascanius, son of the Trojan wanderer Aeneas. Alba eventually came to challenge Rome itself and the two cities settled their differences in a combat of champions. The Roman Horatii finally vanquished the Curiatii of Alba, and the story was later immortalized in tragic drama and in painting.

Due south of Albano lies Ariccia, with its central square designed by Bernini. To the north-west is Castel Gandolfo, summer house of the popes. It commands the best prospects of the Alban landscape, looking across Lake Albano and up towards the 950 m (3,124 ft) Monte Cavo.

East of Rome and overlooking the rolling Campagna district surrounding the city, Tivoli rivals the Castelli in charm. Italy has always inspired foreign landscape painters. Indeed, its landscape may be considered to be the originator of all interest in the subject among the artists of Western Europe. This countryside of hills and plains can be found in the background of paintings by Poussin, and to English artists Tivoli was particularly appealing. This may have had something to do with the fact that it mixes the man-made and the natural with such success. The works of man look as if they have grown out of the landscape, while the trees, waters and hills have an engagingly artificial look.

Tivoli was a favourite with the Romans. Horace celebrated it in his poetry and the Emperor Hadrian built himself a handsome villa here. Its features, excavated comparatively recently, included baths, terraced gardens and two theatres. One of these was for dramatic performances and the other, flooded with water, was for mock sea-fights. The Renaissance left us the wonder of the Villa d'Este, its garden studded with fountains and cascades. Here musicians as much as painters found pleasure and inspiration. In the end it is hard to decide whether the Castelli region, with its little country towns, or Tivoli, among its trees and waters, is the lovelier. Both make ideal counterparts to the unforgettable experience of Rome itself.

LEFT *Youngest of Rome's myriad fountains, the Trevi was created in 1762, as an ensemble displaying the figures of Health and Abundance amid nymphs and tritons. To many travellers it offers a traditional Roman memory: it is the custom to throw two coins into the bowl over one's shoulder, the first said to guarantee a return to Rome, the second the fulfilment of a wish. Its waters, the 'Acqua Vergine', were brought here by Agrippa, friend of Augustus Caesar, in 19 BC to feed his monumental baths. About 79 million litres (17½ million gallons) of water a day rumble and squirt over the Baroque statuary group.*

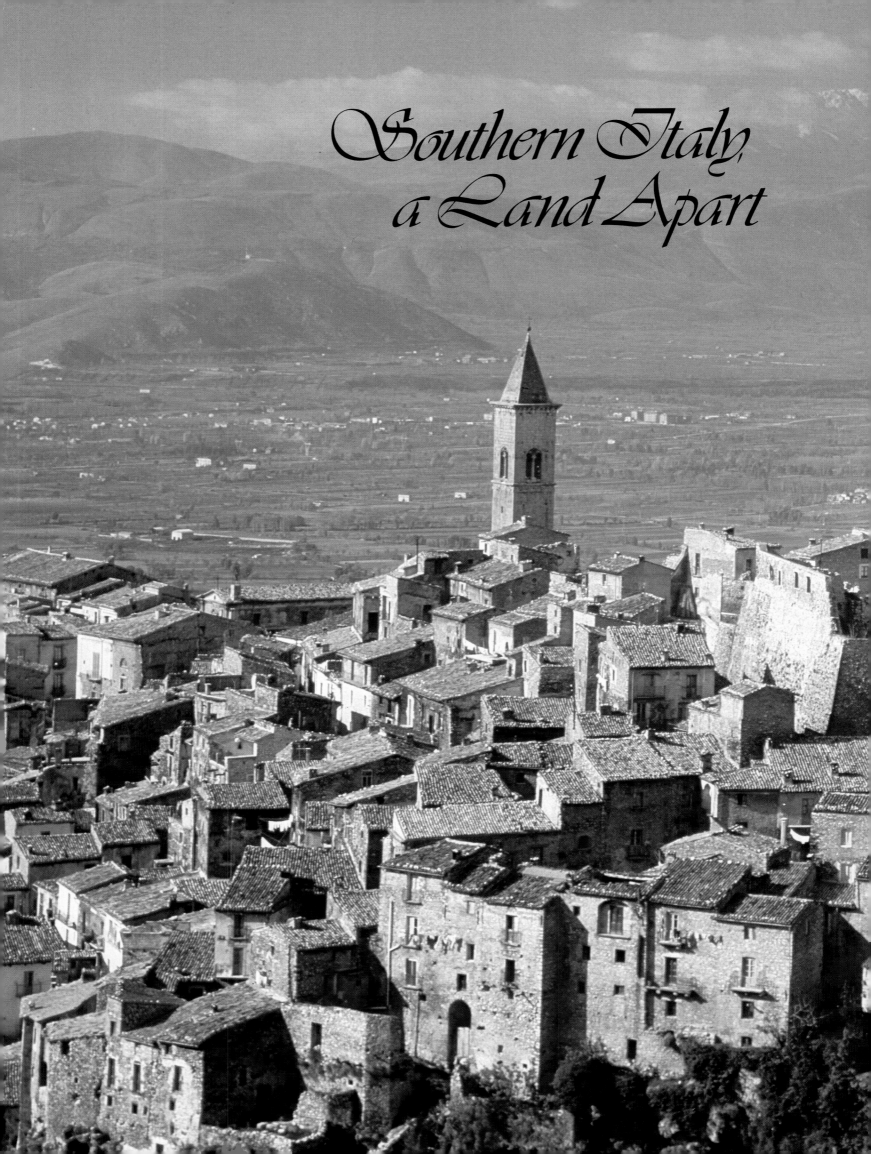

Southern Italy, a Land Apart

PREVIOUS PAGES *The village of Pacentro in the Abruzzi rises up towards the majestic, rugged mountains typical of the region. These mountains, which once sheltered wolves and brown bears, contrast with the sheltered, fertile valley below them, where vines, olives and almonds are grown. Nearby Sulmona is the local market town.*

LEFT AND ABOVE *Two views of Naples summarize the total experience of this bizarre city. Founded by Greek colonists under the menacing shadow of Vesuvius, it unites staggering extremes of magnificence and misery. The extraordinary Italian genius for survival at all costs is highlighted by the vigour and variety of life in the crowded* bassì, *the city's slums. The constant noise and dazzling light, the mixture of gaiety and wretchedness, all impress the visitor to the city. Posillipo, on the other hand, conveys a different Neapolitan image, though just as compelling. This promontory forms part of the Bay of Naples; from it Vesuvius, the Sorrento peninsula, the islands of Ischia and Capri and the city itself may be seen between the garish sea and sky. There are some marvellous excursions possible along this promontory, with splendid views at almost every turn. Farther west the Phlegrean Fields, a volcanic area where hot springs and geysers issue from the ground, are very beautiful. On the other side of Naples there are walks round Vesuvius and a chair-lift to the summit, which is also accessible by foot. The panoramic view from here is, as may be imagined, immense and presents the traditional background to a tourist Italy of lively song and dance. Naples is in fact the centre of the Bel Canto, and the songs, accompanied by guitar or mandolin, reflect the contrasts of life in this city. A Neapolitan song festival is held every September.*

The Italian peninsula has traditionally been thought of as a large leg encased in a high-heeled boot, and we still speak of the 'toe' and 'heel' of Italy. The entire leg, from thigh to instep as it were, was united under a national flag as recently as 1870 after years of bitter struggle. But so late a unification was made at a price. For Italy is clearly still two nations and a host of provinces. It seems as though nothing will ever bring it wholly and successfully together.

South of Rome (or if you are cynical, south of Tuscany), something changes. The change is not necessarily a gradual one; it can be noticed quite suddenly. The rhythms of life slow down, and there is a greater sense of the passing of time. In the early afternoon or late morning the piazza fills with mahogany-faced, stubble-chinned men in baggy brown or blue suits and dinted felt hats. They chat softly and at length with one another. Women are less often seen in public, except in the early evening when the great southern Italian ritual of the *passeggiata* or early evening stroll begins.

The *passeggiata* is not exclusive to Italy, of course. You can see it in differing forms in Marseilles, Valetta, Madrid or Corfu. But its presence is crucial to the rhythm of existence in the Italian south, which is often referred to as the *Mezzogiorno* (meridian). In the late afternoon following work, with many shops still open, the slow, easy amble begins. Up and down, up and down move groups of friends, engaged couples, husbands and wives, bands of children, gangs of students, even whole families. The beat is always the same – a long main street or some broad busy piazza with an arcade, maybe. And for ten who

go walking there will always be one who watches from her balcony. The elderly or infirm take part in spirit if not in fact.

This, as many northern Italians will tell you, is one of the pleasanter faces of the south. Other aspects are not so reassuring. There is a tendency nowadays to romanticize the seediness, apathy and squalor of the region, but this is possibly just an attempt to make a virtue of these drawbacks. 'The problem of the south' is a complex one. It has been created as much by ignorant northern politicians as by a heritage of feudalism and corrupt administration.

During the past 100 years many southerners have emigrated, to northern industrial towns like Milan and Turin, to Switzerland and Germany, to Britain and the Americas. Most have gone in search of a better life in return for hard work. Those who have looked for rich pickings from crime and corruption have done more than most to give the region its bad image, especially among fellow Italians. Partly as a result of this, the north continues to turn its back on what it calls the 'lazy', 'inefficient' and 'dishonest' south. Those who have stayed behind have had to bear this burden, as well as the historical legacy of neglect and oppression.

Yet the beauty of 'heel' and 'toe' endures. The people of the south have often shown themselves to be more imaginative and philosophical in facing the challenge of life than their fellow countrymen nearer the Alps. Under the glare of a fiercer sun, the landscape is bold and sharply defined in the outlines of its barren mountains, rocky river-beds and parched valleys. Not all is arid, however, and places like the Gargano peninsula mingle stretches of forest, pasture land and fertile valleys.

The essence of southern Italy is summed up in the great city of Naples. On its broad bay, with Posillipo at the northern end and the Amalfitana coast stretching south, it lies under the ominous grey form of Mount Vesuvius. It was here in AD 79 that the Roman cities of Pompeii and Herculaneum were engulfed in lava, ash and mud in one of the grimmest volcanic disasters of history. Their remains, progressively excavated since the end of the 18th century, can be visited today and are still being uncovered. A recent discovery was the richly adorned villa of Oplontis at Herculaneum. Paintings of the type that decorate this villa can also be seen in famous houses at Pompeii such as the Villa of the Mysteries and the House of the Tragic Poet. Just as interesting are the smaller finds, bits and pieces of everyday life now preserved in the Naples museum. Things like loaves of bread and baskets of walnuts, surviving from 1,000 years ago, are poignant and evocative reminders of a horrifying catastrophe.

Naples itself has not yet been attacked by Vesuvius, though there were always those who felt that it deserved to be. Victorian visitors like Charles Dickens and William Ewart Gladstone were shocked by its sleaziness and by the people's preference for taking life as it comes, which seemed so very un-English. These aspects prevail today in the life of the cavernous slums of the old city with their strings of washing and overcrowded tenements. Far from being miserable, however, the atmosphere is tense and noisy. The guiding principle is one of survival at all costs. Putting things together to make some kind of a living, taking care of one's family and using influential friends – these are what count. Ambition and success therefore play a large part in the life of the enterprising southerner.

Foreigners know Naples as the home of the pizza, that flat, round dough-base sprinkled with tasty tomato, cheese and herbs. It is also the city of macaroni, not the tasteless English variety but a delicious dish with thick, strong sauces. In a city of such extremes of wealth and poverty, eating has become a ritual. In Naples you notice that people eat in a more obvious manner than normal. There is a great deal of lip-smacking, a more extravagant manipulation of fork and spoon, a more appreciative gulping down of glassfuls of wine.

This sensual attitude comes out in some of the city's other pleasures, chief among which has always been music. Naples has traditionally been one of Italy's leading opera capitals, along with Milan, Parma and Venice. The Teatro San Carlo, built in the mid-18th century, is an opulent temple with tiers of gilded boxes in the familiar horseshoe layout. Composers such as Verdi and Donizetti achieved early success here. Nowadays, amid scandal and confusion, the tradition of good performance somehow continues.

Song, pure and simple, is part of the Neapolitan experience. It was from Naples that a particular kind of popular ditty, accompanied on guitar or mandolin, came to be identified so strongly with Italy. The throaty tenor of some fisherman or stevedore singing 'Santa Lucia' or 'O Sole Mio' summed up the idea perfectly. Apart from the volumes and volumes of Neapolitan songs, some with music by operatic composers, there are a multitude of good singers and fine instrumentalists still found here.

Naples offers the tourist the usual attractions of a great Italian art city, but these are coloured by its very special past. Until 1860 it was the capital of an independent kingdom. This fact is proclaimed in the magnificence of its royal palaces and collections. The Spanish Bourbon family to whom it belonged have been given a worse press than they perhaps deserve. In the 18th century Charles III, for example, took a genuine interest as an enlightened despot in advancing his kingdom in politics as well as technology. Even Ferdinand II genuinely loved his people and his city. He was known as Bomba because of his bombardment of Sicilian ports in 1848 – and because he looked a little like a fat bomb himself. Naples, what is more, had Italy's largest aristocratic class, a host of princes, dukes, marquises, counts and barons. Something of their presence can still be felt in the survival of formalities of manner and custom among the city's people.

The kingdom ruled by the Bourbons was the whole of the 'foot' of Italy. In these wild-looking, barren regions of Basilicata and Calabria we may feel ourselves back in a different era. However well cultivated it is in places, the land seems strangely unmarked by man. Hillsides and mountain tops are bald and jagged. The little towns perched so perilously on their edges hardly look like the work of humans at all. Life here is tough, bafflingly so to northerners, and full of mysterious social categories and superstitions. But the people are tenacious and patient. Their villages were often built as communal fortresses against the danger of siege.

Raiders would perhaps have come from the settlements of Muslim Saracens encamped in these regions in the early Middle Ages. Others might have been in the employ of Norman warlords who would later dominate Sicily. A powerful medieval figure was Frederick II, Holy Roman Emperor and King of Sicily. Called Stupor Mundi ('the Wonder of the World'), he was born at Jesi near Ancona, and never seems to have felt at home outside Italy. He was an elegant poet, a shrewd statesman and fond of hunting. We can still gauge the effect his personality must have made on his contemporaries when we visit places such as the octagonal fortress of Castel del Monte. This is one of several dramatically sited castles in Apulia, the 'heel' of Italy.

Its capital is at Bari, which became a prosperous port under Frederick. Bari still thrives as a maritime and commercial centre, and its old core is particularly attractive. Patron saint of the city is Nicholas, the friend of children and prisoners. As Bishop of Myra in Asia Minor, he was one of the great figures of the early Church. But he is equally memorable for his amazing miracle of bringing together the dismembered bodies of three children, which a butcher had pickled for selling to the townsfolk during a famine. Sailors brought Nicholas's relics to Bari in 1087, and nowadays his feast is kept with processions and a service at sea.

His church is the fine old basilica begun by the Norman captain Roger Guiscard from the remains of a Byzantine palace. Throughout, there are touches of a delicate and imposing Romanesque style. This is seen especially in features such as the marble episcopal throne supported by crouching figures. The pattern of three aisles here is echoed in Bari's cathedral, which belongs to the same period. Both buildings have an awesome grandeur rarely

ABOVE Matera's rocky hillside mingles a huddle of houses and cave dwellings scooped from the soft stone, many of them indistinguishable from the rocks themselves. Many of the streets of the town run close to the roofs of houses whose lower storeys are built into the rock. Houses and stairways overhang one another in an intricate maze of streets and alleys in which one could easily get lost. Matera overlooks a deep gorge, one of very many in this wild and desolate region of Basilicata.

ABOVE RIGHT This street in Pompeii is still lined with the shops of this once busy Roman city on the fertile plain near Naples. In 79 AD a storm of volcanic ash from erupting Vesuvius buried Pompeii, preserving countless intriguing relics of ordinary life. Especially interesting were the various foodstuffs, such as nuts and small loaves of bread, found where they had been left after many centuries. The streets are lined with high pavements and often crossed by stepping stones, as seen here, for the use of pedestrians. Chariot wheels, which have left deep ruts, could still pass through the gaps between them. Excavation only began in the mid-18th century, and about two-thirds of the city have so far been uncovered.

RIGHT Nearby Herculaneum, engulfed in a tide of boiling mud by the same eruption of Vesuvius, was the first of the two cities to be excavated, rather unscientifically, at the beginning of the 18th century.

BELOW *The heavy masonry of Bari's cathedral suggests that it was built not only as a church but also for use as a stronghold. Begun in 1087, it has been reconstructed several times in the course of its history, and is one of the most remarkable examples of Romanesque architecture in Apulia. It is dedicated to St Nicholas. Patron saint of children and the original 'Santa Claus', he lies in the cathedral. The feast of St Nicholas, on 8 May, is celebrated at sea, with people in boats praying before the saint's statue.*

RIGHT *Calabria, the 'toe' of Italy, has a stark, rugged landscape sheltering ancient villages, some of whose inhabitants still speak the Greek or Albanian of refugee ancestors. Pentedattilo, shown here, is the Greek for 'five fingers', an obvious allusion to its rock formations. The Calabrian mountains were renowned as places where violence and brigandage flourished, but nowadays this lonely, romantic countryside is a neglected and forlorn corner of Italy. By contrast, the coastal plain is fertile and fully cultivated.*

found elsewhere in the south and make Bari a place of pilgrimage not simply for devotees of good St Nicholas.

Apulia, or Puglia as it is more correctly called, has superb contrasts of landscape. At Castellana, near Bari, there are impressive natural grottoes, while on the Gargano peninsula beechwoods and mountains mingle above pine-clad coasts. The colours of the south are at their strongest here. The huge limestone plateau was once, apparently, a separate island. It sticks up like a fragment of bone and has herds and flocks on its upper reaches. Today the tourists are starting to visit Gargano in large numbers. But unless high-rise hotels take over, the brilliance and sharp features of this stretch of coast will not be spoilt.

One visitor who loved it was Edward Lear, who went on a sketching tour in 1846. His pictures of the south show scenes that have hardly altered in 100 years. Though he knew Gargano and the dry, rugged 'toe' of Calabria, we have no record of his visit to Lecce. This town is one of the south's many surprises. Local building materials have something to do with it, for the honey-coloured limestone is soft and easily worked. Out of this limestone, Baroque designers employed by the bishop and the civic dignitaries created a swirl of palaces and public buildings. They are airy

and agile rather than pompous. The highlight is the Piazza del Duomo, formed by the grand façades of church and civic buildings.

The east coast is not the only area of remaining beauty, for Amalfi lures us westwards again. Amalfi was once a powerful seafaring republic and a rival of Genoa, Pisa and Venice. That explains the splendour of the cathedral, which mingles, like so much in the south, touches of Arab, Greek and local Italian workmanship. The campanile is like a minaret, and one of the bronze doors came from Constantinople. The surrounding city is exceedingly attractive. Its fertile gardens and growths of citrus, vine and almond often look as if, one day, they will overrun the houses.

On either side stretches the lovely Amalfitana coast. Positano and Sorrento are now a trifle smart and commercial, but the rest has resisted valiantly. The houses and terraced gardens and vineyards sometimes look as though they had been made specially for the clifftops on which they perch. The sea, a vivid blue, has a slick finish to it. Faced with the charm of Ravello, among whose Moorish palaces Richard Wagner composed snatches of his opera *Parsifal*, or with villages such as Vettica and Maiori, we are tempted not to believe in what we see. But in a very southern and direct fashion, it is all there for us to see and to experience.

The Islands: Sicily and Sardinia

Few people arriving in Sicily the proper way – by the night ferry from Naples – are likely to forget the moment they first glimpse Palermo among its orchards and palm groves in the early glow of dawn. For this is also a foreign country. Italian of a kind is spoken here. The first Italian poems were written here. The usual paraphernalia of Italian life can be found all over the island. But such things are simply a veneer, the traces of an occupying power. Sicily exists on its own, and the shifting patterns of history have merely added to its singularity. A Sicilian will always seem to have a more natural right than his Italian counterparts to that local pride that puts a man's province above his country in any list of priorities. In Italy he is a foreigner with an Italian passport. In Sicily he fits easily into that amazing racial and cultural mix that underlies existence on the Mediterranean's largest and most fascinating island.

In some ways Sicily's story seems to encompass the histories and peoples of almost every other territory in southern Europe. The island was of crucial importance to the Greeks, who ruled it from the 8th century BC. Cities like Syracuse, Messina and Agrigento produced a flowering of poetry, science and architecture. The Romans later saw it as a massive granary, a storehouse of plenty to be plundered again and again by corrupt colonial administrators. The Byzantine Greeks left traditions of art and bureaucracy that were inherited by Norman adventurers, cousins of those who, at about the same period, were to conquer England. And between Byzantine and Norman came nearly three centuries of Arab domination which, some say, left the most powerful mark of all.

Others argue that the later Spanish influence can be more obviously felt. French and English also added their contributions. At the court of the 12th century King Roger II, where Greek, Saracen and Jew worked side by side in Palermo, several leading officials, churchmen and civil servants were Englishmen. Many years later a Lancashire man by the name of Whittaker founded the greatest of the wine-producing firms at Marsala. In 1813 the English actually took over the island for a time, and Lord William Bentinck devised a British-type constitution for it.

Sicily, however, has never taken kindly to these foreign intrusions. Nearly all the invaders met bitter resistance. In the 19th century the stubborn independence of the Sicilians showed itself at its best. Ruled from Naples by the Bourbon kings, the people struck time and again for greater freedom. They were the first

PREVIOUS PAGE The 12th-century church of S. Giovanni degli Eremiti is one of many fascinating survivals of Palermo's days as capital of the Norman kingdom of Sicily. Its domes and ornamented masonry suggest a Muslim mosque, and here in the mediaeval city Muslim, Jew and Christian worshipped side by side. The rich and exotic heritage of this culture has left an enduring mark on Sicilian life.
RIGHT Urban grandeur and rural simplicity jostle each other in the centre of Palermo. The city preserves an air of decaying magnificence within its setting of lush fruit orchards, palm groves and tropical blooms. Gothic churches, Byzantine sanctuaries, opulent theatres and statuary stand alongside still-majestic ruins.

RIGHT The workmanship of these columns of the Temple of the Dioscuri (Castor and Pollux) at Agrigento shows the sophisticated taste of 5th-century Greek colonial civilization. This is one of several Doric temples in the so-called Valley of Temples, whose magnificence is best seen by the early morning or evening light, when the stone takes on the mellow colour of honey.

BELOW A total contrast is offered by the enchanting late Romanesque cloister at Monreale, on the hillside above Palermo. Here all the warmth and exuberance of Norman Sicily is conveyed to us in the beauty of filigree relief and sensuous lines, and Arab influence is evident in the decoration of the columns. The nearby cathedral at Monreale is famous for its mosaics, which illustrate the cycle of the Old and New Testaments, and it too shows Arab influence in its decoration.

FACING PAGE Tomato-paste making and other outdoor activities in Noto happen against a stunning backdrop of honey-coloured Baroque churches and a main street of palaces unrivalled in Sicily. The grandiose design of this little town was carried out after an earthquake in the late 17th century.

to rebel in Europe's Year of Revolutions, 1848, though the rising was crushed. Just 12 years later the island was united with Italy following Garibaldi's daring campaign of liberation.

Life since then has not always dealt kindly with the Sicilians. Rule from Naples was corrupt, but rule by kings from the alpine foothills suggested that Sicily did not exist. Neglect and northern contempt were met with surly hostility, mass emigration and the strengthening of those mysterious ties created in village society by the presence of the Mafia. To many people nowadays this is all that Sicily means. Yet the Mafia operates in certain carefully determined areas and cannot be found at all in others. Its activities in the northern Italian industrial cities and, of course, in the United States can be traced directly to roots in the upland villages of north-western Sicily.

What is the Mafia? It is not exactly an organization, nor a system, nor a social group, but very much a state of mind. It was born of centuries of fear and exploitation, of a wish for greater security at any price in an uncertain world. It had its roots in a hunger for respectability, however gained, and in the ability to play

off timid peasantry and remote landlords against one another. We can feel its presence in the huddled hamlets among the bald, deserted hills as much as in the dingy streets of Palermo. Whatever police and government may do, it shows no signs of slackening.

Palermo itself remains one of the most exhilarating places in the Mediterranean. Its grey-suited gentlemen may be sinister, its ruined palaces may look dismal, yet it still appeals because of the bizarre, Oriental exuberance of its buildings and gardens. An Arab town? Yes, perhaps, in the crowded, festering alleys of the Vucirria, or in the Moorish look of some of the Norman palaces and churches. But we can also sense the powerful presence of Byzantium in the golds and blues of mosaic decoration, the finest in Western Europe. And, to confuse us still further, there are buildings in an ornate Gothic style typical of Aragon in Spain, and paintings to match. And in places like the Oratory of the Rosario, hidden in a quiet back street between two shops, we find a burst of wild Baroque in the plaster work of Antonio Serpotta framing a Vandyke altarpiece.

The city is compelling in its mixing of both majesty and wretchedness. Everything here seems mad or overstated in a way that is exclusively Sicilian. There is an enormous circular opera house, the largest in Italy. Not far away stands the equally huge Politeama Garibaldi, a theatre built in the Pompeian style with gaudy pseudo-Roman frescoes. We move from the stiffly formal style of the four fountains in the Quattro Canti to the lavish brilliance of the cathedral of Monreale, high on a hillside beyond the city. This is a unique blend in mosaic and stone of Byzantine, Arabic and Norman styles in Sicilian art. And there is the eerie vault of the Capuchins, where the corpses of 19th-century citizens of Palermo slowly and odourlessly decompose. Preserved by the extremely dry air, some are still dressed in their original top hats and flowered muslin skirts.

Sicily is full of these signs of mortality, warnings and witnesses from her vivid past. The south-western part of the island is scattered with the grandest ruins of Grecian architecture still remaining. Greece itself has little to compare in sheer wholeness and size with, say, the temples of Segesta and Agrigento or the acropolis of Selinunte. Agrigento makes the most potent impression. Its valley holds at least six temples. Of these the so-called Tempio della Concordia is better preserved than the others. Like the southern Italian ruins at Paestum, these substantial traces of a vanished civilization inspired the late 18th-century revival of Grecian design in everything from porcelain to dress styles.

As a total contrast, on the other side of the island we can visit the little Baroque towns of Noto, Modica and Ragusa. The last two are sensationally sited: Modica occupies a deep gorge, while Ragusa occupies a lofty hilltop. Both these boast spectacular churches with twin-towered facades, domes and imaginatively shaped windows and doors. Some of their palaces have a pomp and grandeur that is set off by the little squares and terraces in front of them. But it is Noto that is the biggest eye-catcher of the three. An earthquake destroyed the old town in 1693, and the new one 5 miles (8 km) distant was founded here 10 years later. The result is a country town of true Baroque splendour, of broad streets and extravagant piazzas, with churches, convents and theatres in honey-coloured stone.

North-east of these surprising places lies

the volcanic mountain of Etna. An ascent to the lip of the crater is undoubtedly exciting but 'at your own risk'. Like much of coastal Sicily the volcano's lower slopes are extremely fertile, bearing lemons, figs, almonds and olives and producing good wine. Two cities that grew up in Etna's shadow are Catania and Syracuse. Catania, a busy industrial city, has little to offer the tourist. It was the birthplace, however, of the composer Vincenzo Bellini, whose early death in Paris in 1835 robbed opera of one of its most individual talents. After a period of neglect, Bellini's work has enjoyed a significant revival in recent years.

Syracuse nourished her artists as well, and no visit to Italy is complete without a halt here. The city is really two settlements. There is a sprawling industrial landward complex and a lovely compact old town on a little island. Under the Greeks this city was the island's biggest. Here the tyrant Dionysus suspended his sword over the head of Damocles by a single horse-hair. It was in Syracuse that Archimedes first cried 'Eureka!' as he discovered the principle of water displacement, and he kept the Roman fleet at bay with lethal sun-lenses. In the magnificent theatre hollowed from rock the earliest performance of

Aeschylus's play *The Persians* was given. Aeschylus met his death in Sicily when he was hit on the head by a tortoise dropped from the claws of a passing eagle.

In the old town there is still a delightful maze of rambling streets full of Renaissance and Baroque palaces. These retain their sumptuously detailed façades and their charming little balconies of wrought iron. There is a poised elegance about these houses that gives Syracuse an appearance somewhat similar to the towns of Malta or the Balearic Islands. We seem far removed here from the dourness of a place like Palermo.

This expansive, airy quality is wonderfully echoed in the cathedral. Its tremendous Baroque façade is tacked onto the massive skeleton of a Greek temple. Dedicated to Minerva, this was built in the 5th century BC and was praised for its beauty by the Roman orator Cicero. The internal walls of the cathedral have been scraped away in order to show the existing columns in all their grandeur. Opposite is an excellent archaeological museum. Among its outstanding treasures of sculpture is the famous Venus Anadyomene, showing the goddess rising from the sea. In the Palazzo Bellomo, Syracuse also has Sicily's

Mediterranean ports, brings together the characteristics of a modern harbour, a charming old regional capital, and one of the great cities of classical antiquity. It is really two cities, one a modern industrial area on the mainland surrounding several major Greek ruins which date back to the time when this city rivalled Athens and ruled all Sicily. Among them is one of the largest, best-preserved of ancient Greek theatres. The other is an elegant little town on an island reached along a narrow causeway, full of Baroque palaces and Aragonese Gothic churches.

finest museum. This is a fine collection of paintings, porcelain and *objets d'art* displayed in the setting of a mediaeval palace.

Among the paintings are several by Antonello da Messina, Sicily's greatest master, who flourished in the 15th century. Though there is a strong similarity with Flemish and Venetian styles, his manner is intensely personal. His style seems less at home in the vibrant atmosphere of Sicilian towns. It belongs more to her lonelier places, the hills, orchards, farms and seashores.

This east coast has always inspired artists and writers. Most celebrated in this connec-

tion is Taormina, which faces Etna itself. Taormina's serene beauty has made it more than just 'a sunny place for shady people.' With its fine classical theatre, Baroque fountains and late mediaeval palaces, it summarizes much of Sicily's story.

North of Sicily the various islands of the Tyrrhenian Sea are well-loved resorts. Names like Elba, Ischia, Capri and the Lipari Islands instantly evoke images of brilliant skies and shimmering seas. Capri has welcomed everyone from Tiberius Caesar to Gracie Fields, and its charm lingers on. Elba, between the Tuscan coast and the French island of Corsi-

ca, once sheltered the latter's most famous son. In 1814 Napoleon Bonaparte was exiled here, finally escaping the following year only to be defeated at Waterloo.

Biggest of the Tyrrhenian Islands and still in many ways the most impenetrable, is Sardinia. The very names here have a peculiar sound. Arbatax, Dorgali, Fordungianus, Nuoro – they all seem to carry something belonging uniquely to this island. Its hinterland, mountainous and wild, is notorious as the haunt of bandits whose kidnappings continue unchecked. Perhaps this adds an extra fascination to the place, for the tourists keep on coming. The light and colours are strong, like the scent of the mountain brushwood. The people, descended from Phoenicians, Romans, Arabs and Spaniards, mingle qualities associated with all these races. In remoter villages, local costume is still worn and the language spoken is a barely recognizable form of Italian.

Apart from the island's capital at Cagliari, the most striking man-made things here are the strange, conical fortress-houses known as the *nuraghi*. These are to be found on hills and hillsides all over the island. People familiar with Scotland will be reminded of the stone *brochs* of the northern and western isles. This parallel is natural enough for the *nuraghi* were probably built in the same prehistoric period as the *brochs*. Whatever the secrets of the people who lived in them, these houses have come to symbolize the essential 'difference' so characteristic of Sardinia.

LEFT *Sardinia is only part of Italy in an official sense, and, indeed, it is partly self-governing today. In almost every respect it is uniquely itself, with its own dramatic beauty of landscape with wild mountains and rugged, high plateaux, and its fiercely independent people whose character reflects the harshness and austerity of the terrain around them. The central uplands are notorious for the brigandage still carried on there, and the remoteness of the villages ensures its survival as part of Sardinia's heritage. Many Sards speak an extraordinary language which has inevitably been influenced by the successive nations that have occupied the island, from the Phoenicians and Romans in ancient times to the Pisans, Genoese and Spaniards more recently. Sardinia was united with Italy in 1861.*
The Sards have a wealth of traditions, and here villagers take part in one of the many religious feste. *They still wear their magnificent costumes, particularly on such occasions. The women's costume includes a lace mantilla, embroidered blouse and long pleated skirt, and the men wear gaiters and a cap known as a* beretta. *The most important festival is the Sagra di Sant'Efisio at Cagliari, the island's capital, held every May to commemorate the martyrdom of a Roman general who was converted to Christianity.*

RIGHT *A street leading down to the harbour in the village of Tellaro creates an unmistakably Mediterranean scene, and makes an appropriate farewell to the land and people of Italy.*

Index

Figures in italic refer to illustrations.

Acknowledgments

The publishers would like to thank the following individuals and organizations for their kind permission to reproduce the photographs in this book:

Special photography by John Sims.

Gaetano Barone: 30 below left, 38–39 below, 54 right, 68–69, 71, 82, 84 left; Robin Bath: half title, 27 left, 28, 51 inset, 73; J. Allan Cash Ltd: 26, 54 left, 80 left, 95; Bruce Coleman Ltd: (John Sims) 14 left, (Jessica Ehlers) 72; Editoriale Gemini: 62–63; Susan Griggs Agency Ltd: (A. Woolfitt) Foreword, (Michael Bays) 39 above; Sonia Halliday Photographs: (Jane Taylor) 27 right, 46 left, (F. H. C. Birch) 90 below; The John Hillelson Agency Ltd: (Burt Glinn/Magnum) title page, (Herve Gloaguen/Viva) 21 inset, (Fred Mayer) 29, (Ted Spiegel) 53, (Dennis Stock – Magnum) 66–67, (Leonard Freed – Magnum) 91, (David Hurn – Magnum) 94; Angelo Hornak: 20–21, 24–25, 41 right, 48–49, 58–59, 59 inset, 74–75; Alan Hutchison Library: (P. Goycolea) 13; James Mortimer: endpapers; The Photographers' Library: 8–9, 76–77; Pictor International, London: 10–11, 30–31, 36–37, 40–41, 60–61, 64, 65, 70, 80–81, 83 above, 83 below, 88–89, 93 right; Pubbli Aer Foto: 12 below; Spectrum Colour Library: 86–87; Tony Stone Associates Ltd: 17 above right, 50–51, 55, 63 above right, 78–79, 84–85, 90 above, 92–93; Zefa Picture Library (UK) Ltd: (Bob Croxford) 22–23, (Harald Mante) 56 above left.

SALUMERIA

CARNI SUINE I. Q. - tel. 27801

LATTE SCREMATO

SPECIALITÀ TOSCANE
Capocollo
Finocchiona
Pancetta Arlotta
Spalla Cruda
Prosciutto Crudo

Bevete
Coca-Cola

CAMPARI

CAMPARI

CAMPARI